# THE
# GREATEST
# QUEST

# THE GREATEST QUEST

## BLAINE AND BRENTON YORGASON

Deseret Book Company
Salt Lake City, Utah

No part of this book may be reproduced in any
form or by any means without permission in writing
from the publisher, Deseret Book Company,
P.O. Box 30178, Salt Lake City, Utah 84130.
Deseret Book is a registered trademark of
Deseret Book Company.

First printing October 1987
Second printing February 1988
Third printing November 1988

**Library of Congress Cataloging-in-Publication Data**

Yorgason, Blaine M., 1942–
    The greatest quest.

    I. Yorgason, Brenton G.   II. Title.
PS3575.O57G74   1987        813'.54        87-22373
ISBN 0-87579-114-X

*For those who earnestly seek*

# Contents

# Authors' Note

Shortly after the beginning of World War Two, Floyd Weston and four of his college friends set out on a quest to find the one true Church of Jesus Christ. Armed with a list of seventeen points that they had compiled, they began visiting different churches, searching. Although later separated from each other by the war, in the next few years four of the five young men, by differing routes and under varying circumstances, found and joined one particular religious denomination. The fifth didn't join because he had been killed in the South Pacific.

This book is the fictionalized account of that quest.

# Acknowledgments

We acknowledge the help of Floyd Weston, Sheri Dew, Ron Johnson and Guy K. Lester in the preparation of this manuscript. We would also like to thank our father, J. Gayle Yorgason, for helping document the forty-two evidences of the true church.

# PART ONE

## The
## Present

# CHAPTER
# 1

When the STAT call came over the speaker, I was almost thirty minutes beyond my shift, and was just finishing the cast on a particularly difficult fractured wrist. Normally I leave casting to the technicians, but the young girl with the fracture had serious problems. No specialists had been immediately available to set the crazily misaligned bones; and so, as Emergency Room physician, I had ignored time and procedure and stayed with her from X-ray, finally completing the task.

I smiled at her; wiped her small, oval, tear-streaked face; did my best to defer the almost obsequious gratitude of her parents; and fled to the scrub-room, where I hastily cleaned up

"Marilyn," I then said into the hospital exchange, "this is Doctor Altman . . ."

I got no further, but listened with exhausted mind as Marilyn, a dear friend who almost single-handedly ran Emergency from her cubicle of an office, spoke in anxious tones of the accident victim who was even then being rushed into Emergency O.R.

"Paramedics report cervical spine injury and apparent

spinal damage," she stated quickly. "According to their report, there are many lacerations and contusions, and possible internal bleeding. They're worried about the head, though the man does seem alert."

"Sounds bad," I said, feeling real sympathy in spite of my exhaustion. "But Marilyn, I went off duty almost half an hour ago. Doctor Hooker is here, and Doctor Thomas is on call—"

"Joe, the man keeps asking for you."

"For me?" I asked, surprised. "But who is he?"

"We don't have a name yet. What do you want me to tell the charge nurse?"

For a moment I hesitated, thinking of the date I had made with my youngest daughter, Marcie. She had brought her college roommate, and best friend, home for the holidays, and we were all planning on an enjoyable evening together.

All their lives I had had the tendency to put my children off, and lately I had vowed that no longer would I let my work interfere with my family. And this might be only that—an interference.

On the other hand, it might also be a friend, someone I would surely want to at least acknowledge. If I did nothing else, I could reassure whoever it was that he was in good hands. That would take only a few minutes, and I would still have plenty of time to meet my daughter and her friend, and then spend the evening with them.

"Marilyn, I'll see him. And call my daughter Marcie, will you? Tell her there's an outside chance I'll be late for our date."

"You're a good man, Joe. And Marcie will understand. She's too much like you not to understand."

I accepted the compliment for my daughter and myself, hung up, and hurried down the corridor into one of the longest, most memory-filled evenings I have ever spent.

# CHAPTER 2

A
ll right," I said quietly to the charge nurse as I pushed toward the hive-like activity of Emergency O.R. "What do we have on him?"

"His neck, Doctor Altman. We've no X-rays yet, but there seems to be severe trauma on the cervical spine, and the patient feels no pain or other sensations below his neck. Doctor Hooker says he's quadriplegic, at least, and is in spinal shock. Doctor Hooker is with him now, and I think I saw Doctor Hammond coming in."

I immediately wondered why on earth the man felt that he needed *me,* and could not imagine an answer — not unless he was an old friend or acquaintance.

"Do you have an identity?" I asked the nurse.

"Yes. His name is Deltano. James Deltano."

James Deltano. *Jamie Deltano!* My surprise was so great that I almost halted in mid-stride.

"Are . . . are you certain of the identification?" I asked quickly.

"Well, that is the name I was given."

"Thank you," I muttered as I hurried, almost panic-stricken, down the hall.

Now my mind was truly awhirl. An old friend, and was he ever! Jamie Deltano was one of the two or three closest associates I had ever known, though I hadn't seen him in at least a year. Friendships do that, though. They're on-again, off-again sorts of things, where people move in and out of other peoples' lives. I've noticed, though, that if friendships are true, then no matter how much time passes between seeing each other, it is as though the last visit had occurred only a day or so before. And that was the way my friendship with Jamie Deltano had always been. Close. Personal. Truly I loved the man as much as if he had been the brother I had never had.

When at last I looked down at the still form on the gurney, I felt myself growing almost faint. It was Jamie, there was no doubt of it. He had the same large head and wide forehead that always, to me, signaled unusual intelligence. The same wiry body that seemed filled with nervous energy. The same delicate fingers that years before had wielded the chalk and written such intriguing things upon a long blackboard we had stowed in my apartment at college.

"Jamie?"

For a moment there was no movement on the still face of my friend.

"Jamie, this is Joe Altman. Can you hear me?"

Finally Jamie's eyes flickered open, rolled slightly, and focused in recognition.

"Joe?" he whispered. "Joe, what's . . . what's a good guy like you doing in a place like this?"

I smiled at Jamie's never-ending, wonderful sense of humor.

"Slummin', Jamie. It's Friday night, you know. Isn't that what we always did?"

Jamie tried to smile but couldn't quite manage it. And somehow I knew then that he understood how badly he had been injured.

"Am . . . am I going to make it, Joe?"

"You will if I have anything to do about it, buddy. I thought you knew how to drive."

"I do, Joe. It . . . it was that blasted Ferrari. I knew I shouldn't have leased it . . . but you know me . . . "

"Yes, I do know you. Thank God that I know you. Where's your wife and family?"

"They're at home, in Chicago. I think. Let them know about this, will you?"

"Of course I will. And I want you to know, my friend, that you'll have the best help available. How do they say it? You've come to the right place?"

Turning, I looked meaningfully into the eyes of my friends, Doctors Keith Hooker and Hugh Hammond. Each of them nodded in silent response. Then, stepping past the covey of medical help that surrounded the gurney, I grabbed the telephone.

"Marilyn, call the Riverside Country Club and get Dick Thomas down here immediately. Tell him it's . . . it's special, for me. Then we need a neuro-surgical team, and fast. Get an internist and an orthopod here, too. And STAT them."

"All right, Joe. By the way, I missed Marcie. She is likely already on her way here."

"That's fine, Marilyn. Send her in when she gets here. Also, get hold of the Deltano family, in St. Charles, Illinois. Since Jamie's divorce I don't know exactly where Deanna is, but some of his family should still be around. If you can't find any of them, then call Bill or Helen Benac, same city. They're friends and church associates, and they'll be able to track some of them down. And Marilyn, you're great. Thanks."

Hanging up, I stepped back to Jamie's side, where I did what I could to comfort him while the others worked. Jamie was on oxygen, and Keith was doing some preliminary pin-pricking on his extremities. Sadly, he was getting absolutely no response. Hugh cleaned up the worst contusions and abrasions, and did a little quick stitching where it was needed most, avoiding the head.

And I—I just watched and ached and prayed. To be perfectly honest, in all my years of practice I had never felt so helpless.

"Joe," Jamie whispered, "I can't feel anything."

Startled that he was still so lucid, I looked down. "I know, Jamie," I said gently. "You have some trauma in your cervical vertebrae."

"Say it straight, Joe. My . . . my neck's broken, isn't it. Am I paralyzed?"

"Yes," I hedged, "at least temporarily."

"Oh, dear God . . . "

"I'm sorry, Jamie."

Suddenly my friend's eyes sparkled. "Well, at least I'm not in much pain. A man's got to be thankful for what he can, doesn't he?"

"He does," I said, smiling in spite of myself, while two of the nurses looked strangely in my direction. I'm certain that to them our conversation sounded inappropriate. But it wasn't, for that was Jamie—honest, straightforward, humorous; but never, absolutely *never* beating around the bush.

By this time I was pretty much an emotional wreck, and I knew that I couldn't go into O.R. with Jamie.

Stepping away from his side, I realized that Doctor Thomas had just arrived. "Dick," I said earnestly as I took his arm, "if there was ever anyone to whom I owed everything good in my life, this would be the man."

Dick nodded. "We'll do what we can, Joe. It'll be uphill, though. I'm sure you can see that."

"I . . . I know. The thing he has . . . he has going for him, is his unusual alertness. That, and his will to live. He is an incredible man. We go back a long way together, you know."

"Let's talk while we're walking, Joe. We've got to get him up to O.R. Are you going to scrub?"

I took a deep breath. "I . . . I don't think so, Dick. I was, but I don't think I can. Not yet, at least. I'm too close, and my mind keeps seeing memories instead of reality. Maybe in a little while . . . "

"Daddy?"

Spinning around, I was surprised to see my daughter standing behind me.

"Hello, Marcie."

"Daddy, who is he?"

"Come here. He's awake, and I want you to say hello."

Quickly, Marcie and I stepped to Jamie's side.

"Jamie, this is my daughter, Marcie. Hon, you remember Jamie Deltano? You've met him before, but I think its been awhile."

Marcie nodded. "Hi," she said timidly.

"Hello, my dear," Jamie whispered. "You . . . you are even more beautiful than I remember. Must have gotten your looks from your mother. Joe surely couldn't have been responsible."

Marcie giggled just like she had when she was tiny and was complimented by my friends.

"You've got a lot of room to talk," I growled roughly. "As I remember, you won the 'Ugly Award' at Southern Cal."

"That's only because you didn't enter," Jamie said, smiling wanly. "At least that's what Susan always said."

"Are we ready?" Dick interrupted gently. "We've got to get this man into O.R."

"You coming, Joe?" Jamie asked.

"I . . . no, I'm not . . . not yet. In a little while, maybe. God bless you, my friend. I love you."

"I love you, too," Jamie growled fiercely. "And God *has* blessed me, Joe. Especially with a friend like you. Later, as the k-kids say?"

Jamie smiled weakly, I touched his face gently with my fingers, and then the technicians wheeled the gurney into the hall. Marcie and I stood by while the group hurried away, helplessly watching. And I didn't mean to weep. I certainly hadn't intended to. But as I saw Jamie being wheeled way, the tears came, unbidden. And I found myself holding my lovely daughter and trying to regain control of my emotions.

"I'm sorry, Marcie."

"Don't worry, Daddy. I know how much you love him, but we just have to trust in God."

"Marcie," I replied as I wiped my eyes and led her toward the doctor's lounge, "I know that. It's just that Jamie has done more for my happiness than any other man alive."

"I remember the stories, I . . . Oh, Daddy, I almost forgot. Let me introduce you to Arlene Calkins. She's the best roommate a person could ever have."

"Hello," I said to the tall blonde girl who stood shyly behind my daughter. "It's a privilege meeting you, Arlene. I'm sorry it must be under such emotional circumstances."

"Don't be sorry, Doctor Altman," she replied quickly. "I've heard so much about you. I mean, Marcie has told me, and others, too, about how you care so much . . . Well, I'm sounding silly, but I really am happy to meet you."

"Thank you."

"Daddy, will Jamie be okay?"

"I . . . I don't know. I hope so. In a little while I'm going up there, but I've got to sit down for a few minutes, clear the cobwebs out. You don't mind if I break our date, do you?"

Marcie smiled. "Daddy, you know better than to even ask that. But I'll tell you what—why don't Arlene and I sit with you for a few minutes, just to keep you company?"

"Are you certain you don't mind?"

"I certainly don't!" Arlene declared with a smile. And feeling the warmth of that smile, I knew why my daughter had grown so close to her.

Moments later, seated comfortably in the doctor's lounge, I found myself thinking about Jamie, and wanting very badly to talk about him.

"I've told you about him before, Marcie, when you were younger . . . and when your mother was alive. If you'd like, and with your permission, Arlene, while we're waiting I'll tell you the story of how I came to meet . . . Jamie Deltano."

"I'd love to hear it," Arlene replied gently. "I . . . well, I've waited a whole semester to meet you, and—"

"Arlene's very sensitive to things spiritual, Father. Actually, I wanted to tell her your story, myself, but I thought you could really do it more justice. After all, it *is* your story, and I'm just the benefactor."

Marcie smiled, and as she did, I could see again, as I had for years, the beauty of her mother reflected in her countenance. Again I teared up, but this time it was from love—love and sheer loneliness. Susan had died in childbirth, even as Marcie was being born. And after eighteen years, I still felt the pain as though her death had been yesterday. And yet God in his mercy had given me Marcie, a perfect mirror-image of her mother. And for that, as always, I was grateful.

"Thank you, Arlene," I continued, "for indulging an old man in a sentimental conversation. I . . . I had no idea

I would be sharing this experience with you . . . in such . . . such a precarious moment, with Jamie on the operating table. But perhaps there could be no better time. I . . . I would like to tell you about us, about Jamie Deltano, Marcie's mother . . . and me."

Easing back into the soft lounge chair, I propped my feet on the low table before me, stretched my fingers out to relax them, took a deep breath, and rubbed my eyes.

"It was at Southern Cal that I met him. I've told you, Marcie, how I had always wanted to be a brilliant and respected doctor. But the competition was fierce, and the best of all the competition in the school was this kid who kept the whole institution buzzing with his amazing exploits in learning. His name was Jamie Deltano . . . "

# PART TWO

February 28, 1942
to
April 25, 1942

# CHAPTER
# 3

Gentlemen, the deeper that I delve into the sciences of the universe, the more firmly do I believe that one God, or force, or influence, has organized it for our discovery.

"I thank you for your time."

Doctor Albert Einstein concluded his lecture, there was an instant hush in the vast hall, and then the faculty and students of the university stood in unison as they burst into thunderous applause. In the hall outside, the three of us, all undergraduates listening in on the lecture of one of the greatest scientists of all time, were caught with that last amazing declaration. We looked at each other, fled outside ahead of the departing crowd, and walked to my apartment discussing it.

The late May Southern California weather was balmy and peaceful, giving a lie to the fact that our nation was in the initial throes of the Second World War. Wake Island in the Pacific, and Hong Kong, had been taken by the Japanese. Manilla was under siege, Japanese Americans were being rounded up and sent to government camps, and an oil refinery near Santa Barbara had been shelled by a Japanese submarine. And finally the Government had just instituted rubber-tire and limited gasoline rationing, giving the war effort a much-needed boost.

It was a traumatic time, and as young college students we thought much about the war, about living and dying, and about what our futures might hold.

"Do you believe in a God?" Jamie Deltano asked me. "Like the God Doctor Einstein believes in?"

I looked down at my friend, surprised at his question. I was a sophomore at the university, not quite twenty years old, and feeling somewhat inclined toward religion. However, standing just over six feet tall and being fairly broad-shouldered, I also felt that I had pretty good control of my world. Nobody pushed me around, I was moderately good-looking, and I dated as often as I chose to date. I was of at least average intelligence, I had a job that supported my schooling and my car, and I had two good friends. Still, with the blossoming war at hand, I was more and more turning my thoughts toward God.

Of course, my religious inclinations had received some impetus when my mother had died. At the time of her death I had begun to think seriously about the hereafter. But I was quite young then, and my feelings were given little chance to grow. Instead, I spent the next several years being shuffled from one institution or home to another, never really having an opportunity to contemplate religion.

As soon as I was old enough to hold down steady work, I struck out on my own. And I had been on my own ever since, almost six years. In that time I had graduated from high school, bought a car, and put myself through a year and a half of college, studying premed. I had chosen that field not purely because of altruistic reasons, but because I had never met a poor doctor. In short, I wanted to be rich.

Therefore, by that time I had neither an attitude, nor had I lived a life, calculated to teach me a dependence upon God.

"A God?" I said. "Of course I believe in God."

Will Huckstedder, the third member of our group, looked anxiously toward me as he spoke. "You believe in God, Joe?" he asked, surprised.

I nodded soberly.

"Hmmm," he mused. "I suppose that leaves you odd man out."

"You don't believe in a God?" I asked, surprised at his declaration.

"I certainly don't," Will declared. "This life is all there is. Nothing was before, nothing comes after. This," and Will emphasized the word, "is *it*."

"That makes you an atheist, Will," Jamie interrupted quietly. "And I'm *not* an atheist. Among a few other items, I believe most firmly that there is a God—a God who, by nature, is *good*."

I looked at Jamie, then, surprised by his vehemence as much as anything else.

"Then I most certainly am an atheist," Will declared, glaring at Jamie as he did so. "And both of you are fools. Anyone is, who believes that religion bunk about a God, especially one who is good."

I was quiet then, a ripple of uneasy tension lapping at me. Frankly, I was shocked at this unexpected turn in the conversation. Will Huckstedder, a farm boy with a head of dark, raven-like hair as well as a set of muscles that wouldn't end, had instantly and effectively thrown our discussion into a complete tail-spin.

Suddenly Jamie smiled and clapped Will on the shoulder. "Will," he said, "I'm delighted to know how you feel."

"You are?" Will asked, totally surprised by Jamie's declaration.

"Absolutely. Would you like me to tell you why?"

I considered Jamie Deltano's question carefully, for he was our undisputed leader in almost all things. He stood a little shorter than I did, was thin almost to the point of looking starved, and wore dark-rimmed glasses that made him look like an owl. And he was wise like an owl, too. He had a photographic mind that was so good that he could read a page of text, put the book away, and quote it almost verbatim. And even more amazing, he could do it with great accuracy long after he had read the text.

He never studied, at least as Will and I had to study. Instead, he spent his time reading and theorizing and postulating. If one of the learned professors had a question about some element in Jamie's field of political science, or even other areas, they often came to him to resolve it.

It would have been easy for either of us to be envious of Jamie, for we were both just average students. But neither of us felt jealous of him at all, for our friend was that rare, truly brilliant person who had absolutely no sense of self-importance. Instead he was humble in the truest sense of the word, and so open-minded that he would tackle literally any problem — and then set out, using his amazing mind, to solve it and share the solution, no matter what the answer. It was this very trait that brought about what followed.

"Sure I would," Will replied to Jamie's question.

"Very well," Jamie said, turning very serious. "Gentlemen, would you care to hear a short tale?"

We both nodded, whereupon Jamie sat himself on the grass and bade us sit beside him.

"For over a year," he began, "I have been on a quest, a very private quest, to learn who, or *what*, God is. I have many reasons for making this quest, but none of them would likely affect either of you. Thus I will leave them undeclared.

But be that as it may, I have learned much over the past year, though I must admit that God himself has eluded me — I have failed to find him."

Both Will and I grinned at that, but if Jamie noticed it, he gave no indication. Instead he continued in complete seriousness.

"I have examined the causes of this failure and concluded that one of them, perhaps chief among them, has been that I am so alone in my search. Gentlemen, I have no one to bounce my ideas off of, no one to listen to my theories and to help me correct them."

"What about the chaplain?" Will asked.

"I've thought of him," Jamie replied slowly, "and reluctantly rejected him. You see, he is already steeped in the religious tenets of his faith and cannot be objective. I need objectivity, a fresh approach, if I am to succeed."

"Why?" I asked.

" 'Why' is an easy question to ask, Joe, but a difficult one to answer. For one year I have been studying the Bible and bits and pieces of works that have been written about it; histories and commentaries and so forth. My studies have convinced me that there is indeed a God, but that *no one* I have met knows how to find him."

"And you think that you might learn how?" Will asked incredulously.

"I don't know, but I feel that I need to try. Would you gentlemen be interested in joining forces with me, at least temporarily?"

Miserably I plucked at the grass, tossing bits of it toward a large root that had humped out of the earth nearby. "Jamie, I don't know. I've got so doggone much to do . . . "

"Joe, I won't ask you for a lot of time. I just need your perspective. The same thing goes for you, Will. In simple terms, I propose that we all three become an experimental group—our own case study, if you will. Joe, let me ask you a question. If you believe in a God, do *you* know where to find him?"

"I . . . ah . . . I guess in church," I responded.

"Have you ever seen him there?"

"Well, no, but. . . . "

"Have you ever heard him?"

"No, but doggone it, Jamie. . . . "

"Have you felt him, then?" Jamie persisted.

"I don't know," I whined in frustration. "How should I know where . . . or *how* to find God? And I sure don't know what he feels like!"

Jamie rose to his feet and clapped me on the back. "Well, Joe, if God does exist, it seems to me that we ought to be able to find him. What say we start looking?"

Well, I was astounded, and the more I thought about it, the more astounded I became. *Look for God?* The very idea seemed absurd, ridiculous. But one look at the seriousness of Jamie Deltano's face, and I knew he meant it. Literally, my brilliant friend had determined to find God.

"What do you say, gentlemen? Are you with me?"

I looked at Jamie and could see his enthusiasm. He was almost bouncing with it. I looked then at Will and grinned and shrugged my shoulders, and he grinned back. Instantly we two had our own silent agreement. We would play along, at least for the time being.

"I'm in," I said.

Will pulled himself smoothly to his feet. "Me too, up to a point."

"Fair enough," Jamie grinned as he led out toward my apartment. "Now Joe, do you believe that God has given mankind any teachings?"

"Sure he has."

"And would I be right in stating that those teachings are properly called religion?"

I grinned. "That's how I'd put it."

"Okay," Jamie continued as we walked toward our rooms, "are God's teachings sacred?"

"I guess I'd call them sacred."

"I wouldn't," Will declared, "and I don't agree with this whole line of reasoning."

"Of course you don't, Will, and we understand that. But don't worry about it. You are our control element, the one who looks, with objectivity, at everything we conclude."

"*What?*"

"Listen, Will, you don't need to convince us that you are an atheist. We believe you. And we aren't trying to convince you that God lives. But for the sake of this experiment, we would like you to assume the role of our control element. You watch us carefully, remember our stated beliefs, and make certain that we don't come to false conclusions about those beliefs. Do you think you can do that for us?"

"So . . . you don't want me to argue with you," Will stated, sounding puzzled. "I'm only to watch and referee whatever it is that you are going to conclude. Is that correct?"

"Exactly. But our conclusions must be within the limitations of our expressed beliefs. In other words, the issue will *never* be, 'Is there a God?' That there *is* a God is one of our constants. Fair enough?"

Will nodded his puzzled agreement, and it would be years before I ever realized how thoroughly and effectively Jamie had neutralized Will's possible antagonism. Even more importantly, he had cemented Will's support and friendship, and that turned out to be valuable indeed.

"All right," Jamie continued as we gathered into my apartment, which was large and was destined to become our central gathering point, "the second constant must be: Jesus Christ is the Son of God. Joe, do you believe that?"

I nodded my head. Will smiled paternally as though he knew a great atheistic secret that neither of the rest of us even suspected the existence of, and Jamie continued.

"Very well, then, we have one constant left to determine. Does the Holy Bible contain God's sacred word?"

Once again, I agreed that it did.

"Good. That will conclude our discussion for today. Joe, do you have your Gideon Bible there in your dresser?"

"I sure do. It hasn't moved since the day I arrived."

"That sacred text must surely be important to you," Will teased, absently flexing his muscles as he folded his huge arms.

I laughed with embarrassment, and Jamie took the Bible.

"Joe, keep this out for reference. Let's meet again tomorrow night. By then I think I can have my notes together so that I will have something to show you. Shall we say . . . eight o'clock?"

We both agreed, and Jamie departed, leaving Will and me very much in wonder. Jamie was dead serious; we both knew it, and both of us were astounded at the thought.

But we were also excited. Jamie was a remarkable man, and he was about to lead us down a remarkable path; one which, for us, would become our greatest quest.

# CHAPTER
## 4

I'll tell you this," Jamie declared as we sat together the next evening, "this project is much bigger than I imagined when I started it a year ago."

I laughed. "I could have told you that. The Bible is always a big project. I've never met anyone who has read it clear through."

"My mother did," Will declared. "She was always reminding me of what it says. In fact, the Bible is the only book I ever saw my grandfather read, and he read in it every night of his life. I can't even guess how many times he read it clear through."

Jamie nodded. "You're right, Will. Many people read it; some just as casual literature, and others devouring it as the word of God. But the thing that surprises me is that I can't just skim through the Bible and understand it, like I do so many other texts. I have to ponder it, over and over, before the things I have read begin to fall into place. But in the past year I have read much of it at least twice, and I discovered some information that seems vital. Joe, did you get that blackboard cleared with the head resident?"

"I got it cleared," I replied. "But I haven't picked it up yet."

"Could you get it now?"

"Sure." I smiled and then arose and made my way down the hall to the room where the huge blackboard was kept.

Steering the blackboard back into my room, I found both of my friends laughing over some joke. Then as they made way for me to bring the long blackboard into my room, there was even more laughter.

"Is that your new bed, Joe?" Jamie chided.

"No," Will chorused, "it's his new car. All he needs is a motor and he can drive it around selling advertising."

"Great idea," Jamie agreed. "It'll have to be a diesel truck engine, though, because it's so big."

"A *big* blackboard for a big project," I declared as I worked it against the wall behind my bed.

"Big?" Will teased. "What are you going to write on there, Jamie? A book?"

"Maybe." Jamie grinned as he took up a stick of chalk. "If I do, will you read it?"

"Sure. But only if you autograph it."

"Even if it's about religion?" I asked quickly.

Will looked at me, grinning. "That might change it a little."

"Actually," Jamie said easily, "it wouldn't. Joe, you forget that Will is our monitor. For him to control our experiment, he'll need to be as familiar with our theories and hypotheses as we are. Right, Will?"

Our atheist friend nodded reluctantly, and Jamie stepped back to the blackboard, his chalk held in the air before him.

"Will the class please come to order?" I quipped.

"Hear, hear," Will agreed, and I could tell that we were all feeling just a little anxious and uncertain about what we were doing. We sensed that something bigger than life was about to begin, but truthfully, not one of us, including Jamie Deltano, had any idea how powerful and all-pervasive what we were doing would one day become.

"Okay," Jamie began, looking at us, "I have found that there needs to be a fourth constant, a given fact upon which we agree."

"Uh . . . what were the first three?" I asked sheepishly. "I forgot already."

Jamie smiled and wrote on the board as he spoke. "That God exists, that Jesus Christ is his Son, and that the Holy Bible contains his sacred word. Remember?"

I nodded. "I do now. So what's the next constant?"

"That Christ, when he lived, established a church — *his* church."

"I don't know about that one," I said uneasily.

"In that case," Will declared, "it can't be a constant."

Jamie hesitated thoughtfully, his gaze upon the floor. Finally he looked up and smiled at Will.

"Actually, Will, you're right. It can't. If we're going to conduct this experiment according to the scientific method, we need to state this as our hypothesis. And we should, for this is the conclusion I have come to, and I want to prove it."

"Come again?" I queried. "I'm not sure I follow you."

"Well," Jamie explained, "I set out to learn who God was, and I have come to the conclusion that I cannot know him until I am somehow united with the church that his Son apparently established for that purpose. Obviously, I can't unite with it unless I can recognize it, and I can't do that unless I can prove that such a church exists. Therefore, we need to present this existence issue as a hypothesis, something we need to prove."

"That is," Will interjected, "if you can. Personally, I think your hypothesis is untenable and unprovable."

"We know what you think, Will. And if you're right, we'll find out. Meanwhile, remember that you agreed not to be negative . . . "

Jamie then turned to the blackboard and wrote out these words:

HYPOTHESIS:
WHEN CHRIST CAME TO THE EARTH, HE ORGANIZED OR ESTABLISHED A STRUCTURED RELIGION — HIS CHURCH

"What you're saying, then," I stated, "is that you think Christ really *did* organize a Church."

"That's correct. But remember, Joe, as I explained yesterday, this project is too big for me to do alone. We've all got to roll up our sleeves and dedicate ourselves to it, or we'll never complete the experiment."

"We never will anyway," Will said, grinning. "And I'm sorry if that sounds negative. It's just how I feel."

Jamie looked soberly at our atheist friend. "You may be right, Will, but speaking personally, I've at least got to try."

"But *why?*"

Again Jamie was silent for a moment, thinking. "My friend," he said at length, "I have a philosophy of life. It is why life has meaning to me. If I don't follow it, then living means nothing, and I become nothing."

Now we were both listening carefully, for I don't think either of us had ever heard Jamie speak so intently or so personally.

"What *is* your philosophy?" I asked bravely.

"You already know part of it," Jamie replied, smiling at me. "God lives, and he is good."

"Yeah, I remember you said that. Is there more?"

"Well, because God is good, the more I learn about God, the better I also become."

"Which is why you want to conduct this experiment?"

"Partially. Next in my philosophy is this: Truth comes from God, and it will always be truth, regardless of a person's lack of understanding, disbelief, or ignorance. My quest is to find all truth. And that ties back in with becoming a better person."

"Is that your philosophy then?"

Jamie smiled. "No, there is more. Are you sure you want to hear it?"

We both nodded, and so Jamie continued.

"I believe that man is affected by many things as he becomes who and what he is. But *always*—always he has the power to affect, use, control, or harmonize with all things that affect him. In other words, man always has the power to be an actor on the stage of life; not just a re-actor.

"More succinctly, I believe that man is created in the image of God, and that he has the God-given ability to direct his thoughts, control his emotions, and ordain his own destiny. As I said, he is the actor in his life, not simply the re-actor.

"I feel that living the dogmas taught by Christ is a dynamic, living, growing experience. Those dogmas are universal, simple and enduring. But they do not come alive unless they are lived.

"And finally, gentlemen, I believe in prayer and the miraculous power that God grants when we pray for it."

Jamie stopped and took a deep breath. I am certain that he was aware that he had stunned us with his ideas, but I doubt he knew how deeply his thoughts would come to affect me personally. Of course I didn't know it then, either. In fact, I hardly understood the words he had uttered. I think Jamie knew that, too, for with his next breath, he summarized in more simple terms.

"That is my philosophy," he declared. "As you can see, it all boils down to one thing: God is the most successful being in all creation. I too want to be successful. I can become successful by following God's advice and learning about him. Or I can ignore him and his dogmas and choose failure for myself. I alone have the power to decide if I will be successful, as God is."

Will and I were quiet, thinking. But I was the one who finally spoke.

"Jamie, I don't think I agree with you."

"Why not?"

"Because I don't see that God and success are linked, as you do."

"Yes?" he asked, encouraging me to continue.

"I . . . uh . . . well, you men don't know much about me, but I have been kicked around for most of my life. I'm tired of that. I'm tired of always being broke, and of having to scratch for every dime I ever get. To me, success is becoming wealthy, and that is my most important goal. Frankly, I don't see how that has anything to do with religion, or with finding God."

"It may not," Jamie said, "but let me ask you a question or two."

"Fair enough," I responded, meanwhile aware that Will was enjoying this immensely. He could see that I was nervous, but so would he have been if Jamie had been about to pick his brain.

"Joe, how old are you?"

"Almost twenty."

"At what age do you expect to be wealthy?"

"Thirty-four."

Will whistled and teased me a little, but I held my ground. "Listen, you toad, I've got college, med school, an internship, and a residency. I'll be thirty-three when I finish all of that. Within another year after that, I'll be set. So back off and watch me roll it in."

"Those are good plans," Jamie agreed, grinning along with Will. "But what happens, Joe, if next week you roll your car and lose both your arms? Then what?"

"Then . . . I guess I do something else," I declared defensively. "It won't matter, though. I'll still become wealthy."

"Suppose your spinal cord is severed, or suppose you suffer minor brain damage?"

"Jamie, that isn't going to happen!"

"How do you know?"

I twisted a little, but truthfully, Jamie had me. I *didn't* know. I didn't think such a thing would happen, but who could declare positively that it wouldn't.

"All right, you win that round. But what does that have to do with God?"

Jamie smiled. "Maybe nothing. But Joe, suppose that it was God's will for you to become a doctor and to become wealthy, and you *knew* that. Could such an accident as I have described, which would stop you from your goal, actually happen?"

"I . . . I don't suppose so. But Jamie, God doesn't care whether I become a doctor or a tree trimmer."

"He may not," Jamie declared softly. "But what if he does? Or, what if he cares not so much about the work you do, as about the kind of life you are living?"

"I don't . . . understand."

Jamie smiled. "All right, think of this. God wants you to be righteous, to keep the commandments. Am I right?"

"Yes . . . "

"Why does he want those things?"

"I don't know. So I can get back to heaven, I suppose."

"Very good," Jamie declared. "Now, does God *really* want you back in heaven?"

"I . . . I suppose he does."

"I'm *sure* he does. Now Joe, if God, who wants you back in heaven, can see that with your wealth you have become proud and wicked and aren't going there, do you suppose he might take away your wealth so that you would repent?"

Dumbly I stared at my friend. "To tell you the truth," I replied slowly, "I've never thought of that. But it makes kind of a screwy sort of sense, when you think of it like that."

Again Jamie smiled. "It does. Do you see, Joe, how God might, in just this one way, have a great deal to do with a man's financial success?"

"Yeah. And taking it the other way, if I keep the commandments, then God won't see any reason to keep me from becoming wealthy."

I grinned widely, and Jamie and Will both laughed. "That would be correct," Jamie declared, "if those were the only variables. Of course, there could be many other ramifications that I haven't even mentioned, probably that I haven't even thought of. But let me say this. To me, success is becoming the very best of what God wants me to become. I may be wealthy, I may not. It doesn't really matter. But I really do want to do what he wants me to. And to learn what that is, I need to find him. Now do you see why I must pursue this issue?"

"I think so," I stated. "But—"

"Joe, until I heard Doctor Einstein yesterday talking about God's organizational abilities, I had never even considered that someone else might be on the same track I have been on. But I had the impression that Doctor Einstein believed that because God was organized, then Jesus Christ also had to be organized. If he doesn't think that, at least I surely do. And that being the case, Jesus Christ must surely have established a literal church or organization. I proposed that we work together because I would truly like your help. I also think that what we learn will help the two of you as much as it helps me. However, if you fellows would rather not be involved, then I'll continue the search myself."

Quickly, Will and I assured Jamie that we wanted to be a part of what he was doing.

"Good," he said sincerely, and I felt certain that he was relieved that we would accompany him during his great quest.

"Jamie," I stated, "you wouldn't have formulated that hypothesis if you hadn't found, in the Bible, some evidence that Christ had created a formal church organization. Am I right?"

Jamie smiled at me, tossed his chalk into the air, caught it, and wrote EVIDENCES OF A STRUCTURED CHURCH under his hypothesis.

"You're right, Joe. I did find something. And that something ought to be here on earth now, just as it was when Christ organized it. In his epistle to the Ephesians, Paul said that there was one Lord, one faith, one baptism. Well, gentlemen, as you know, there are literally hundreds of faiths, dozens of interpretations of who the Lord is, and many different kinds of baptisms. What we are looking for is the original thing, the 'one' in all categories that Paul spoke of.

"As I said, we will be looking for a religion that is organized just as Christ organized it when he was here."

"Wait a minute," Will said, holding his hands up. "Just because Christ did something back then doesn't make it right today."

"Good point, Will. What do you think, Joe? Was Christ perfect, or wasn't he?"

"Well," I answered, suddenly remembering a Sunday School lesson from my early church-going. "Actually, if we are accepting the premise that the Holy Bible is the word of God, then the book of Hebrews answers that question."

As I spoke, I thumbed my way into the New Testament, feeling an excitement that comes always, so far as I can determine, when sharing a rare gem of wisdom with another person.

"Here it is," I exclaimed, "in the fifth chapter of Hebrews, verse 9. In speaking of Christ, the writer says that *being made perfect,*' he, meaning Christ, became 'the author of eternal salvation unto all those that obey him.' "

"Good," Jamie punctuated. "I think that, if the Bible is going to be our source of knowledge, then we must accept *literally* and *in context* what we read within its pages."

"That being the case," I summed up, "we can agree that Christ *was* perfect, and so what he established during his mortal ministry would also be perfect."

"Yes," Jamie concurred, "and that leads us to the next conclusion we must reach as we determine evidences for his Church."

"Don't say it," Will interrupted. "Let me see if I can guess where you're headed. You're saying that if Christ *was* perfect, then he *is* perfect. And if we are going to find his true religion today, we must find the church that fits what he did two thousand years ago."

"Precisely," Jamie replied. "This is quite a foundation we're laying, isn't it."

"I don't know," Will questioned uneasily. "This is deep swimming for me, especially when I don't believe that Christ was any more than a strong and effective teacher."

"Your time will come, Will," Jamie said reassuringly. "If we're going to either confirm our hypothesis or prove it false, we have to establish our premises for launching our investigation.

"Anyway," he continued, "let's stay on track. Joe, you

were reading in Hebrews chapter 5. Flip over to chapter 13 and read verse 8 to us."

Feeling an unusual sense of mounting excitement, I quickly thumbed my way to chapter 13 and then read, "Jesus Christ is the same yesterday, and to day, and for ever."

"Okay," Jamie concluded. "In simple words, if we accept the fact that Christ was perfect, and that he is unchanging, then what he did back then would be no different than what he would do now."

"Let me see if I can boil all this into one pot," I said, taking a deep breath, stretching my legs out, and intertwining my fingers behind my head.

"Go ahead, Joe. Summarize."

"What we're doing here is setting out on a quest for discovery. We're going to find out, through reading in context the words of the Bible, what the Savior's church should contain, *if* there was such a structured form of worship."

"Yes," Will interjected, "and *if* there is a God. And *if* he came to earth and formed his church, then you must scour the scriptures and then form a blueprint of what his church would contain today, *if* in fact he *has* a church here today."

"That's right, Will," Jamie mused. "And if all of those premises fall into place, you might even believe with us."

"Who knows?" Will sighed. "It'll be an uphill battle, though, because of what I've been through."

There was quiet in the room as each of us seemed to share the same instant discomfort. I could tell that Will had some pretty serious things on his mind, and yet I didn't want to intrude on his privacy. Even Jamie was unsure of how to proceed, and so we just sat there, hoping Will would take up the slack he had inadvertently placed in our conversation. The silence worked, too, because finally Will cleared his throat and spoke.

"Actually, fellows, I used to believe there was a God . . . a *good* God, as Jamie says. I even used to pray. My family were all God-fearing people. But that's the problem."

"What's the problem?" I asked.

"You all know that I come from the wheat fields of Kansas. That's where my muscles got a leg up on each of yours," he smiled. "I had to *work* to survive in my younger days."

"Now wait a minute," I blurted. "I've been on my own—"

"Joe, let me finish for you. You've been on your own since you were twelve, you've slept in boxcars and hobo jungles, you walked eighteen miles to school every day, through sixteen-foot snow drifts, wearing shoes with holes in them, and that was only in the summertime. In the winter, things *really* got bad. Am I close?"

For an instant I was upset, and then I saw both Jamie and Will grinning, and I knew things were okay. They understood what I had gone through, and they still felt comfortable teasing me about it. That gave me a wonderful feeling, and as I grinned back at them, I suddenly felt a sense of warmth, a sense of belonging, that words are unable to articulate. I just knew that I loved those two guys, and I would have gladly done anything for either of them.

"Anyway," Will continued, "my family farmed, as they had done for several generations. But then one day a storm blew up, a terrible storm that spawned tornadoes in three different states. The radio warned us that we might be in danger, so Father came in from the barn and gathered Mother and the five of us children together. Then we all knelt in prayer.

"Father prayed and asked God for protection for our farm and for our family. And I had faith, too. I just knew that God would protect us.

"But," he concluded, his voice breaking as he spoke,

"we hadn't even finished that prayer when a tornado ripped through our farm, destroyed our barn and most of our crops, and then tore apart our house. My baby sister was killed, and so was my faith. That day, even though I was only fourteen years old, I became an avowed atheist."

The room was again silent, and both Jamie and I were wondering how, given the same circumstances, we would deal with such a horrible blow.

"Are you sure you can blame God?" Jamie asked softly.

"No, I can't blame God. That's why I know there isn't one, especially a good one. If there was, he would never have allowed such a terrible thing to happen — especially after we had prayed for his intervention."

"Well," Jamie sighed, "I can surely empathize with your feelings, Will. I'm glad you shared them with us. But on the other hand, from my perspective, God doesn't always seem to be in the business of protecting. Instead he is usually teaching. He oftentimes allows tragic things to happen because they teach such powerful lessons. That's part of what makes him so good. He even allowed his own son to be crucified. And though he knew that Christ's sacrifice would be eternally good for mankind, he still grieved from the depths of his heart while it was happening."

"He doesn't sound like a God I want to know," Will said firmly.

"Maybe as you come to know him better, that will change," I stated quietly.

"Okay," Jamie said, breaking the spell as he placed his chalk back on the board. "First evidence of Christ's original church. Are you ready? Here we go . . ."

# CHAPTER
## 5

A true church must believe that the Holy Trinity are three separate persons."

"*Separate persons?*" I questioned, suddenly confused by Jamie's declaration. I had always believed in the Holy Trinity, a profound doctrine of three in one and one in three that made the Godhead into a huge, powerful, single force.

"You have a problem with that, Joe?"

"I . . . uh," I gulped. "You bet I do. 'Separate' is wrong, and 'persons' is wrong, too. How can you degrade the idea of God by describing him as a person?"

"*You* just did," Jamie replied quietly.

"I did not! I said that he was . . . "

"Joe," Will said, laughing quietly, "listen to yourself. *He* is a personal pronoun. So is *him*. In your last two sentences you used both personal pronouns."

"Well, big deal!" I stormed. "Those are only words, and you know it."

"That's correct," Jamie agreed, "words that, in all cases, refer to individuals. But allow me to let you off the hook.

When I said persons, I meant individuals, beings, entities, or Gods. I certainly did not mean to degrade any of the three Gods by calling them persons on the same level as we are."

"I'm glad to know that," I stated, "but there you go again; calling them separate. They aren't, I mean he *isn't*, not unless he wants to be."

"What do you mean, Joe? See if you can articulate what you are saying."

Quickly I looked around, decided that neither of my friends were making fun of me, and so began. "All right. The Holy Trinity is one God with three attributes: the Father, the Son, and the Holy Spirit. Each attribute is part of God, and all, blended together, *is* God. If he needs to do something as the Holy Spirit, then that happens. If he needs to do something as the Son, that happens, too. And the rest of the time he is the Father, God, and that is always so. As I once memorized, the Holy Trinity consists of three entities which are one spirit substance."

"Well, I don't believe that," Will snorted. "What you just spouted is the biggest pile of nonsense I ever heard."

"What religion were you, Will?" Jamie asked quietly.

"Pentecostal. And I'll tell you something—if there was a God, you would be right about him, Jamie. He and Christ and the Holy Ghost must be separate. Nothing else makes any sort of sense at all!"

Surprised at Will's sudden outburst, Jamie and I were both silent.

"Well, I mean it," he stated, defending himself. "Joe, let me ask you—do you pray?"

"Sure I pray. I mean, I used to sometimes, when I was little."

"Silently, by yourself?"

"That's right."

"Okay, when you prayed, who did you picture in your mind that you were praying to?"

I grinned, feeling a little silly. "I . . . I always saw this sort of all-knowing, gray-haired old man."

"What about you, Will?" Jamie asked quietly.

"Me? I . . . I . . . well, I figure any more that he's just a figment of my imagination. I told you that already."

"Yes, you did. But you made a very good point. You gentlemen should know that I am Roman Catholic. Before your churches ever came around the corner, my church was old and steeped in the doctrine of the Holy Trinity. If anyone has the right to believe what Joe described, I do. But the trouble is, I'm just like Will used to be. I can recite all the trinity liturgy I want, but when I pray, I always see a compassionate, white-haired old man.

"That's why this past year, when I read about the baptism of Jesus, I began to wonder. If they are but one essence, then how in the world could they be in three places at the same instant?"

"What? Jamie, sometimes —"

"Listen, Joe. It's right here in your Bible, which as you remember we all agreed to accept. Matthew 3:16-17 says: 'And Jesus, when he was baptized, went up straightway out of the water: and lo, the heavens were opened unto him, and he saw the Spirit of God descending like a dove, and lighting upon him. And lo a voice from heaven, saying, This is my beloved Son, in whom I am well pleased.'

"In Mark, the first chapter, it says essentially the same thing, and the third chapter of Luke agrees but adds the interesting detail that the Holy Ghost came in a bodily shape *like* a dove. In other words, this bodily form of the Holy Ghost came softly down like a dove might come."

"How do you know it means that?" I asked.

"It isn't hard, Joe. It seems clear to me; but to make

certain, I went to the library and read interpretations of several biblical scholars. One or two didn't agree, but the majority saw it just as I do.

"What it all amounts to, my friends, is this: Jesus was coming up out of the water after being baptized, the Holy Ghost was descending upon him in a bodily form like a dove might do, and God the Father was in heaven, speaking his pleasure at his Son's baptism. *Voilà!* Three separate entities."

"So, what about the doctrine of the Trinitarian God?" I asked quietly. "I believe it's true."

"I know," Jamie answered quietly. "I always have, too, until I read those scriptures, and I'm pretty troubled about what I have been feeling since then. However, my discomfort impelled me to research it out, and what I found has made me feel even more uncomfortable than before. But good came, too, I believe, an additional conviction that the three Gods are indeed separate beings."

"I'm not sure I want to hear this," I stated quickly.

Will laughed nervously. "I think I do, but I can understand why you wouldn't. It's a lot easier to think you've been right than to admit that you haven't been. And now you know how I've been feeling. If you always believe, life can be pretty comfortable. To suddenly discover an error, especially in one's basic religious understanding, is enough to make a person bitter."

"It is," Jamie agreed, "unless you can find something that is better—more true. And that, gentlemen, is what our threesome is all about. Now, let me tell you what I learned about the Trinitarian God."

Will and I nodded and agreed to listen, and so quickly Jamie scribbled more notes on the blackboard.

"First, the doctrine is manmade. It was formulated under the Roman emperor Constantine in the fourth century so

that Christians could pray to a God they knew and understood. Constantine, a non-Christian until just before his
death, reasoned that since the Christians were so powerful,
his empire could use their united strength. But that was the
trouble. Christians *weren't* united. Some thought Christ
was human and not divine; some thought he was divine
and not human; some thought he was both; some didn't
know; some took the philosophies of the Mithric and Hel-
lenistic cults and intermingled them with Christianity; and
so on.

"So Constantine called a giant council in the East, in
A.D. 325, and there the learned men assimilated all these
varied forms of doctrine into a single creed about Christ,
the Holy Ghost, and the Father. This was called the *Nicene
Creed*."

"In other words," Will declared, "the church suddenly
had a God made by a committee, just as a giraffe is a horse
made by a committee."

We all chuckled, and then Jamie continued.

"Essentially, Will, that is the way it worked. But the
churches in the West felt left out of this council, so another
was called at Calcedon almost a hundred years later. They
adopted a new creed, nearly the same as the one Constantine
had overseen, and that creed formulates the doctrine of the
Trinitarian God that we have all blindly accepted and believed."

"Are you telling us," I questioned, "that there isn't any
scriptural evidence that the idea of a Trinitarian God is
correct?"

"Not anywhere, Joe. I've looked. And I'll tell you something else. As I've analyzed my understanding of that doctrine, it simply isn't rational."

"What do you mean?"

"Just this. The Trinitarian doctrine teaches that God

is visible and invisible all at the same time; that he is everywhere present and nowhere present at the same time; that he is so big that he fills the entire universe and yet is so small that he can dwell within my heart at the *same time;* and so on. My rational mind completely rejects such doctrine as nonsense. Doctor Einstein based his belief on scientific organization, and the Trinitarian doctrine is the most unscientific, disorganized compilation of nonsense I have ever studied.

"In other words, as I said, it isn't rational. Personally, I think that Christ's church, *if* it exists, ought to be rational."

"That seems pretty final," Will stated then.

"It is, at least in my opinion."

"In summary," I said slowly, "you're saying that if we are to find this 'correct' church, it must believe and teach as a doctrine that God the Father, God the Son, and God the Holy Spirit are separate and distinct entities."

"Correct, Joe. Furthermore, though the Holy Ghost is spirit, God and Christ have tangible bodies of flesh and bone."

"Bodies? Come on, Jamie. You can't—"

"Joe, read here in Luke, twenty-fourth chapter, verses 36 through 39."

I took my Bible, turned to the reference, and read: "And as they thus spake, Jesus himself stood in the midst of them, and saith unto them, Peace be unto you. But they were terrified and affrighted, and supposed that they had seen a spirit. And he said unto them, Why are ye troubled? and why do thoughts arise in your hearts? Behold my hands and my feet, that it is I myself: handle me and see; for a spirit hath not flesh and bones, as ye see me have."

"Thank you, Joe. Now, would you now agree with me that Christ had a physical body following his resurrection?"

"It certainly says that," Will declared for me.

"Yes, it does. And it was important enough to him that he protected it. Remember when Mary saw him in the garden following his resurrection? He told her to touch him not, for he had not yet ascended to his Father. You see, that body was very important to him.

"Now think about it. Would Christ capriciously dispose of that important body after going to so much trouble to take it up in the resurrection? Of course he wouldn't. The very idea is absurd."

"All right, Jamie. But what about God the Father?"

"I believe he must be the same, Joe. Jesus himself declares that he is in the express image of the Father. And of course in Genesis we are told that the Gods created man in their own image and likeness. Obviously they are alike. Besides, thinking rationally, why would the Son have a body of glory while the Father would not?"

"I . . . I don't know."

"I don't either. Such a thing isn't reasonable. That's why I am sure that the Father and the Son are similarly endowed with glorified bodies."

There was silence then, while each of us pondered the strange thoughts and ideas that our quest was already fostering.

"Gentlemen," Jamie finally said with a smile, "this is enough for tonight. I have three papers to prepare for Professor Browning that I haven't yet started; I have a lab assignment due tomorrow; and as I recall, there is an intersquad ball practice that begins in fifteen minutes. That I *don't* want to miss!"

With a shout of agreement Will rose to his feet and followed Jamie from the room.

I was left alone, pondering Jamie's scrawls in the upper corner of the chalkboard. Strange ideas, those. I had never thought of such things, and I didn't know how I felt about them. But as I prepared to go to work, my mind and my eyes drifted frequently to that blackboard, and I found myself wondering.

Was Christ a separate being from his Father? Was the Holy Spirit distinct from either of them? Did they have tangible bodies? And were they even real at all? Jamie certainly thought they were. Understandably, Will didn't believe any of it. I was kind of 'iffy' about it, and I didn't even have a valid reason for my feelings.

So did I really want to make this quest, as Jamie called it? Suppose Christ did have a church. So what? Would that really make any difference in my life?

Who was I? Why was I putting myself through this torture of self-examination? What purpose did my life really have? Sure I wanted to be rich, but as Jamie had asked me, then what? Or suppose it never happened, and I died on my way to work or something. Where would I go then? Or would I even go anywhere at all? I didn't know, and my mind reeled with the multitudes of questions that churned back and forth through my consciousness.

"Lord," I muttered as I did up my bow tie and headed past the blackboard for the door, "if you really are there, please help me to know if it's as important as Jamie seems to think it is."

And with that stumbling effort at praying, I set out for my work.

# CHAPTER
# 6

A postles and prophets?"
I was leaning against the counter of Johnny Anderson's Flying "A" gasoline station, waiting through a momentary lull between customers. Two weeks had passed since my feeble attempt at prayer. I had received no answer that I could recognize, and I had about decided to give it all up. And I would have, too, except that Jamie had been giving me some of the most interesting historical information I had ever learned. That alone had kept me going.

"That's right," I said to my dark-haired boss, who was in his small office closing out the receipts for the previous shift. "Do you think there are any apostles and prophets alive today?"

"Well," he laughed, "I know that Jesus called Matthew and those other fellows to be apostles, but good grief! You can't expect that *anybody* could still be here after all that time. I mean, that's two thousand years ago!"

Now I laughed with him. "I didn't mean that exactly, Johnny. I don't expect that Matthew or any of the rest of them would still be here in person. I even read about when Matthew died, and it wasn't very many years after Christ's crucifixion. He was killed with a halberd or battle-axe. What I meant was, do you think that *somebody* here today, no, twelve somebodies, could be apostles, exactly in the same way that Matthew and the others were apostles?"

Johnny scratched his head in perplexity, his greasy hands oiling further his long dark hair. "Beats me, Joe. You'd think if any of those fellers were here, we'd have heard about them."

"That's what I told my friend," I replied as I scanned the dark street out front, wondering if I'd have many customers that night.

"What'd he say?"

"He said they'd just be normal men like us, and we'd likely not notice them at all."

Johnny laughed. "I'd sure like to see an apostle with greasy hands like me. Most ministers I've met don't know the first thing about real work."

"You know," I said, looking at my boss, "my friend said the same thing. He said the original apostles had all been hard workers; fishermen, tax collectors, and so on."

"Tax collecting is *work?*" Johnny quipped.

I grinned. "I guess the Jews were as unhappy about that profession as we are. But that's what Matthew was. A tax collector. Anyway, Jamie Deltano, that's my friend—he says that if there are real apostles today, they'd likely be about the same hard-working type of men who were made apostles by the Lord himself."

Johnny thought for a minute, punched a few numbers into his adding machine, totaled it out, and scribbled the figures down. "I don't know," he said as he stood up and gathered together the receipts and money. "Seems sort of far-fetched to me. But if you find any of those apostle fellers,

Joe, I'd like to hear about them, maybe even meet them. That'd really be something—a church-man with greasy hands."

He laughed and walked out, I watched until his red taillights disappeared up Columbia Lane, and then I was alone with the night and my thoughts.

Apostles and prophets. What a crazy idea! Still—

Reaching down, I took up my briefcase and opened it upon the counter. Then I removed my notes, taken from the growing number of scribblings upon the blackboard in my room, and spread them out.

Jamie's list of points or evidences had grown to an even dozen, and according to him there was no end in sight. Almost a third of the blackboard was full, and he was actually talking about finding another board. I had told him he'd need to find another room to put it in, and he hadn't been troubled by that at all.

But Jamie was really into this search, especially now that he had given himself direction. I think he studied that blackboard more than I did, even though it was staring me in the face, night and day, as it stood along the wall of my room.

The bell suddenly clanged, and, looking up with a start, I saw a young woman pulling her new '41 Chevrolet up to the inside pumps. Hurrying out, I took her order, began filling the tank, and washed the windows of her car while I waited for the tank to fill.

Meanwhile, she climbed out of her car and walked inside, and I found myself watching her, admiring her trim form. "She's new here," I said to myself. "At least she's new to my shift. I wonder if she lives around here, or if she's going to school, or what? Oh, wow! Look at that hair. It's gorgeous! And I surely do like the way she carries herself. And take a look at that figure! Whooowee! I wonder . . . "

"Two dollars even," I announced casually as I walked into the station where she was waiting. I was doing my best not to stare at her, but there was something about this woman that I found terribly attractive, even compelling.

"All right," she smiled. Then, while she reached into her purse and handed me some money, I made out her receipt. And though I still did my best not to stare at her, I was losing the battle, and losing it badly. I simply could not keep my eyes off her.

"Do you think they'll decide to ration our gasoline here in the West?" she asked.

"Probably," I told her. "It'll be tough for a lot of people. But if it helps the boys overseas, then I think they'll do it."

"Are you a student?" she suddenly asked, changing the subject.

"Uh-huh. S.C. Going to be a surgeon, I *think*."

I emphasized the last part, about only thinking I was going to be a doctor, and she laughed. "Is premed what you are studying here on the desk?"

I looked down at the counter, strewn with my notes. "No," I said, feeling a little silly though not knowing why. "It's just some religious stuff."

"Religious? Are you thinking of the ministry as a back-up career in case you don't make it in medicine?"

I could see that she was serious, not teasing, and so I decided not to be offended. "Not hardly. A friend of mine, some kind of crazy genius, is doing a study on finding what he calls the 'true church.' I'm just sort of helping him do it."

"My, my," she declared teasingly, "a *true* church? Don't all churches think they are true?"

"I guess a lot of them do. But Jamie — that's my friend — he thinks that if it is going to be a true church, that it ought to be organized the same way that Christ organized it anciently."

The young woman was thoughtful for a moment, and I continued to stare at her, transfixed by her beauty.

"That makes sense," she said slowly, "though it does create problems."

"It . . . does?"

"Well, I think so. I don't know very much about churches other than my own, but I do know that they are different from each other. They all think they are right, too. If your friend's assumption is correct, then there are going to be a lot of unhappy ministers and parishioners."

"That's right," I agreed, feeling a sense of joy that this woman would want to spend time in conversation with me. I mean, at that moment I cared not at all what we talked about, just so we talked. That our subject happened to be religion was simply an added benefit that I had yet to discover.

"Uh . . . for instance," I declared, continuing her point so that I could keep her there until I had learned her name. "Luke . . . uh . . . chapter 6, verse 13, says that Christ called twelve of his disciples, or followers, and named them apostles. Then in Ephesians chapter 2, verses 19 and 20, Paul says that Christ built his church upon a foundation of apostles and prophets, himself being the chief cornerstone."

"Do you believe that?" the young lady asked as she looked up at me.

"I . . . I guess. Those statements are right there in the Holy Bible, and I believe the Bible. What stumps me is, where do I find such people today? Apostles, I mean."

"What happened to the original apostles?" she asked then. "I've often wondered that."

"I used to wonder about that, too. My friend found out, though, and it's pretty awful."

"It is?"

"Yeah. I've got the notes right here. Do you really want to know?"

She nodded eagerly, and so I read them to her.

"Judas, of course, committed suicide. Phillip was scourged, imprisoned, and crucified. Matthew was slain with a halberd or battle-axe, apparently in India. He may also have been crucified and beaten first. James the Less was beaten and stoned by the Jews, then had his brains dashed out by a fuller's club."

"Oh, how terrible!"

"Yeah. Those Jews didn't like Christians, I'll tell you that. And here are some more that they didn't like. Matthias was stoned at Jerusalem, and then beheaded. Andrew and Thaddeus were crucified at Edessa. Mark was dragged to pieces in the streets of Alexandria. Peter was crucified upside down, in chains, in Rome. Paul was also killed in Rome, beheaded by the order of Nero. Thomas was slain by a spear in India. Luke was hanged on an olive tree in Greece. Simon Zealotes was crucified in Britain. It is not known what happened to Barnabas, and John was boiled in oil, miraculously escaped, and was banished to the Isle of Patmos. Apparently there is no record of his death."

The young woman stood in stunned silence. "My goodness," she exclaimed. "Those poor men."

"I agree. Those gentlemen had a pretty bleak future, once they became apostles."

"I don't think I'd ever want to be one."

I laughed. "Me neither. But as far as I can tell, neither of us will have to worry much about it."

The girl laughed with me, then, and I was suddenly aware of how incredibly beautiful her eyes were. I don't know why I hadn't noticed it before, but they sparkled with dancing light. Maybe it was because her laughter brought that out, and I hadn't really watched her laughing until then. That's why I hadn't noticed it.

But that was what did it for me. Her eyes. I was smitten, from then until forever, by her beautiful dancing eyes.

"I . . . I . . ." I stammered, suddenly at a loss for words. "I . . . my friend found another scripture, uh . . . in the book of Amos. It's about prophets. It's . . . it's in chapter 3, verse 7."

"What does it say?" she asked seriously, seemingly unaware of my own stuttering and love-struck behavior.

"The prophet says," I repeated, taking a deep breath, " 'Surely the Lord God will do nothing, but he revealeth his secret unto his servants the prophets'."

"That's in the Old Testament, isn't it?"

"Yes. That means it was spoken a long time ago."

"Do you think it still applies today?"

"Jamie, my friend, thinks it does. He showed us where it says that God is unchanging, which is how I think of him, too. That means if he's going to do anything with people today, he's still going to do it through prophets."

The young lady looked at me, and again I found myself drowning in her unbelievably striking eyes. They were a deep hazel, with light green or yellow highlights, and they seemed much larger than any eyes I had ever seen before.

"Do *you* know any prophets?" she asked.

"I . . . heck, no! I can hardly even make one."

"Ouch!" she winced at my dumb attempt at humor. Then her oval face suddenly creased again with a smile, and at that instant I knew that I never again wanted to look into another pair of eyes. Given the right luck, hers would last me forever.

"Gosh," I blurted foolishly and without any hesitation whatsoever, "you have the most beautiful eyes I have ever seen!"

"I do?"

"Yeah, I mean . . . What . . . what is your name? I mean, I hope you don't mind if I ask. Do you?"

"Even if I cared, it's too late to stop you, isn't it?"

Surprised, I looked at her, and I could feel the red

climbing up my neck to my ears. "I . . . I guess. Only I didn't mean to . . . I . . . "

"Susan," she said, her eyes dancing again with those lovely lights. "What's yours?"

"Joseph Altman."

"Hello, Joseph Altman. Are you always this concerned with religion?"

"Me?" I blurted. "I don't think so. I mean, well, lately I just can't quit thinking about it. But religious? I . . . I . . . "

"I hope you are," she said, totally surprising me by her declaration. "I think that young men who are religious would make much better husbands and fathers than those who are nonbelievers."

And at that instant, with her declaration ringing in my ears, I made up my mind that I would be religious for the rest of my life. Of course, I didn't know what that would come to mean, but I didn't care very much, either. The vow, for all its suddenness and spontaneity, was nevertheless real.

# CHAPTER
7

Susan, whose last name was Bartholomew, rapidly became the focal point of my life. Or, she became one of two focal points. The other was Jamie's rapidly expanding material. In six week's time he had dug and compiled and recorded, and our conclusions had grown and expanded, until they filled most of the huge blackboard.

"Joseph," Susan asked one night as we were bowling together, doing our best to squeeze what was rapidly becoming a romance in between school and studies and work, "have you found anything more in your experiment?"

"Well," I said, stretching my legs out and leaning back, "Jamie's found fifteen points of doctrine in the scriptures, I think mostly from the New Testament, that will be found in Christ's church. He calls them 'Evidences of the True Church'."

"Fifteen? That's a lot of evidences, Joe."

"I'll say. I just hope all this research does some good."

"What do you mean?"

"I mean, what if we can't find a church that matches

all these things? What if that church doesn't even exist any more?"

"You think it *doesn't?*"

"Susan," I said as I rose to my feet and took up my ball for the last frame, "do you think I'll roll a strike this time?"

"You might. Why?"

"In my opinion, the chances of my rolling a strike — and I've only rolled two in my life and not one in the last eight or nine games — is much greater than our finding a church that has all fifteen of those characteristics. Maybe my chances are a thousand times better, or even a million. In other words, I'm beginning to think that such a religious institution just doesn't exist."

"It's that impossible?"

"Yeah, like me and a strike."

"Well," she smiled, "roll it and let's see what happens."

I smiled back, nonchalantly stepped to the line, and let go of the ball. And to my absolute non-amazement, the ball slid into the gutter.

"See," I said with exasperation as I sat down to remove my shoes, "that's how impossible it is."

"Joseph?"

"Huh?"

"May I see the list?"

Reflexively I reached into my pocket; pulled a folded, yellow five-by-seven card from my wallet; and handed it to her.

"Is this it?"

"Yeah. Jamie made a copy for all three of us. Now let's get out of here. I hate bowling alleys. They make me feel inferior."

Nodding her sympathetic understanding, Susan removed her bowling shoes, her eyes never leaving that card.

I paid for the games, and shortly we were in my battered

old Dodge, driving back to her apartment. Only Susan wasn't talking. She was reading and thinking, and I had seldom seen anyone so intense. She was mentally devouring our list.

"This is absolutely amazing," Susan mused after I had pulled the car to a stop. "I wonder if there really is a religion that has all these things in it."

"I don't know. Tomorrow night we're going to try to find out."

"You are?" she asked, her eyes dancing with excitement. "What are you going to do?"

"The three of us are going to go out and start visiting churches."

"Oh, Joseph, may I come with you?"

I looked at her, acutely surprised at her request. To be truthful, I wasn't excited about going. In fact, I was as nervous as I could be, for I had no idea what we would encounter when we started going to other churches. I had been raised a Protestant, and basically I felt secure in my religious beliefs. But the thought of visiting the Catholic Church, or one of the Pentecostal churches, or any *other* church, for that matter, filled my stomach with more butterflies than could be found on the annual southern migration of the giant Monarchs. Feeling that way, I couldn't imagine that anyone would be as excited as Susan sounded.

"Are you serious?" I questioned.

"I certainly am! Would there be room, Joseph?"

"Well, it all depends. Have you been a good girl? I mean *really* good?"

"What do you think?" she asked coyly.

"I think . . . I think *not*."

"Not! Why, what—"

"If you were *really* good, you'd kiss me goodnight and get out of here so I could get to work so that I wouldn't get fired so that I could pay my rent and tuition so that I could get a good job and become wealthy so that you and I could . . . "

"Yeeesss?"

I looked down into Susan's eyes again, her eyes filled with those same consuming, laughing lights that affected me so much.

"N-never mind," I stuttered, alarmed at my own forwardness. "I . . . I don't know, but I can't see any reason at all why we can't get four into this old bomb instead of three."

"Thank you, dear," Susan breathed. And then, before I hardly knew what was happening, she had kissed me softly and was out the door.

"What time?" she called back through the open window.

"Time?" I asked blankly, my mind still whirling from that very first kiss.

"Yes, silly. What time tomorrow night?"

"Uh . . . six-thirty. I'll pick you up at six-thirty."

"Okay. See you then, Joseph. And . . . you know what?"

"What?"

"I . . . I love you, Joseph Altman."

With that Susan disappeared into her apartment, and I think I finally gathered my senses enough to drive safely to work. I don't remember that part too well, though. My mind was filled with thoughts of Susan's words. She *did* love me! She even *said* she did, and I could hardly imagine my unbelievably good fortune.

Trouble is, fortunes have a way of changing, of clabbering up just when they seem so smooth. And at the time, I could hardly have imagined that, either.

# PART THREE

April 26, 1942
to
May 25, 1942

# CHAPTER
# 8

The next afternoon, as I returned home from classes, I experienced one of the greatest traumas of my life. For there, in my mailbox, was my notice from Uncle Sam.

I had been *drafted!*

Thirty days! That was all I had to tie the loose ends of my life together, to somehow complete my final exams, and to determine what was going to happen between Susan Bartholomew and me. And thirty days, I suddenly realized, in which to wrap up the unusual search that had been begun with such hope and determination by Jamie Deltano.

For several silent moments I sat in a stupor, my mind whirling with the frustration, the complete unfairness of it all. I was going to war! I was going to end up fighting the Japanese or the Germans, with whom I had no personal quarrel, and in all likelihood I would never live to reach any of the wonderful goals I had set for myself.

And the war was escalating fast. The six-day, 120-mile Bataan Death March had just concluded. Under Japanese control, ten thousand Americans had started the march.

Fewer than a third of them would be alive two months later. Colonel Jimmy Doolittle's bomber squadron had just bombed Tokyo, however, and many Americans looked upon that as good news. And finally, the Government had just instituted rubber-tire rationing and gasoline rationing coupons, giving the war effort a much-needed economic boost.

It was not a good time for any young man to think of going into the military, and it felt to me like a *terrible* time for my own departure from my normal, well-planned life.

As I sat gloomily pondering all of this, the telephone rang, and Will's voice started to bring me out of my shock.

"Hey, man," he said, "you don't sound so good."

"Yeah. I got my infamous letter today."

"Infamous?"

"Yeah. From Uncle Sam."

"No kidding? You got *drafted?*"

"I did. In thirty days I report to Ford Ord, near Monterey, for basic training."

"Ouch!"

"You said it."

"So what are you going to do?"

"Do?" I growled. "What can I do? I go."

"No," Will said gently, "I mean about school? And about Susan?"

"School I drop out of, Will, as soon as I can arrange some early finals. Susan, I don't know. I've got to talk to her. By the way, do you think Jamie would mind if she came along with us tonight?"

"Does she want to?" Will asked, his voice filled with surprise.

"Believe it or not, she wants to go a lot more than I do."

"Well, as far as I'm concerned, she can go. I'd love to meet her, and that would give me the perfect opportunity.

And I'm sure that Jamie would feel the same. After all, you've talked about her so much that she's become pretty famous, at least among us. I'd say, bring her along."

Will and I visited a little longer, said good-bye, and hung up, and I was thinking with excitement of being with Susan and my friends when I realized that I was no longer worrying about my draft notice.

I grinned at that, and I began to think that if I could forget about it so quickly then maybe it wouldn't be such a bad thing after all. So, by the time I picked up Susan and the others, I was in a fairly happy mood.

Susan was an instant hit, and just sensing that made me ecstatic. Friends are terribly important in a young person's life, and sometimes they have an even greater impact upon his or her thinking than does the person's own family. And so it was with Jamie and Will. They had exerted a powerful influence upon me, and if they hadn't approved of Susan, I might have done something that I would have regretted the rest of my life.

"Say, Joe," Jamie declared, "this woman is something! How'd you ever get her to go out with a lowlife like you?"

He laughed, and Will leaned forward in the back seat so he could get nearer to Susan. "Jamie's right, Susan. The smart move would be to dump Joe right now."

"So I could latch my 'fortunate' hooks into you?" Susan laughed.

"I'll say!" Will exclaimed. "Now that *would* be smart. Most ladies groove on my exquisite freckles."

"Yeah," I agreed. "Like grooving on going over Niagara Falls in a canoe, or like — "

"Enough already," Will protested. "Susan will never speak to me again."

"Not a bad idea," I growled.

"Hey, Joe . . . "

"He's only teasing," Jamie declared authoritatively, easing the tension. "We both are. Susan, I for one am thankful that you have taken an interest in our friend, Joe. You see, he needs a lot of patience and help, and we had about run out of both commodities."

"Not to mention money," Will interjected. "Are you rich, Susan? We hope, we hope?"

Susan turned and looked back at Will. "Yes I am," she replied quickly.

"Wonderful!" Jamie declared gleefully.

"I am seated next to a wonderful man . . ." Susan began in explanation.

"She means me," Will mock whispered to Jamie.

" . . . and I am surrounded," she went on, ignoring Will's humor, "by two other men who must be wonderful themselves to be considered as friends by Joseph Altman. How could a girl ever be more wealthy than that?"

There was an instant silence, and then Will shouted, "Hear, hear!"

"Well, if that's not one of the kindest things I've ever heard," Jamie replied softly.

"So tell us, Susan," he then inquired, bringing it all back around, "why did you want to accompany us on this little trek tonight?"

The atmosphere was instantly serious, but it didn't seem to bother Susan in the least.

"Why?" she asked as she reached over and took my hand. "You fellows, Joseph has told me all about your experiment and has even made for me a copy of your fifteen points. I've begun to read my own Bible looking for those points. I have found some, and I think you are looking for what could be the most important discovery in a person's life. In *my* life, more specifically. In plain words, I want to look, too."

"Do you think there could be a *correct church* here on the earth today?" Jamie asked.

Susan looked over at him. "I don't know, Jamie. I know only that there *ought* to be. And if God isn't a respecter of persons, then there *will* be. With all my heart I would like to find that religion."

"Respecter of persons?" I repeated. "Susan, what do you mean by that?"

Susan looked up at me and smiled. "Here's my reasoning, Joseph. It seems to me that I should be just as important to God as those who lived at the time of Christ. That being the case, why should God give them the privilege of being in his church, and at the same time deny the same opportunity to me, simply because I live *now?* The Bible says that God is no respecter of persons. I believe that; and so it seems logical that somewhere on this earth, there should be the same church that Christ gave to the people anciently."

There was a moment's silence, and then Jamie turned to look at Susan. "Do you realize that you might have just found a sixteenth point?"

"I did?" Susan asked in surprise.

"Certainly. Think about your conclusion, which I believe is accurate, and then extend it. You mention just two groups of people — those in Palestine at the time of Christ, and those here in California, or wherever else people might be today. But if respecting of persons really fits in, and I think that it must, then Christ's church must address the spiritual needs of all people, everywhere on the earth, in all ages of human history."

"You mean," Will asked, "*everybody?*"

"Absolutely. Do you all comprehend what I'm saying? What Susan means? One of the points on our list, for instance, is that baptism would be mandatory for entrance into Christ's church. But there are millions, maybe billions of people, who have never had the opportunity to receive such a sacrament. If God is no respecter of persons, then in some way, through his church, he will provide such opportunities for *all* his children."

"But how is he going to do that?" I asked.

Jamie shook his head. "I haven't the faintest idea, Joe. I only know this: When we find that true church, *they* will know."

We rode along in silence, and then, clearing my throat, I spoke. "There may be a seventeenth point. Let me run this past you before we get to the church. I found this in 1 Corinthians 9:16-18."

"My word," Susan declared, "are you *all* so well versed in the scriptures?"

"Hardly," Will replied with a laugh. "Jamie is, and Joe is doing a lot of looking. As for me, I just sort of stumble along."

"Well," I said defensively, "I read this the other day, and I've been thinking about it ever since. In the passage I am referring to, the Apostle Paul talks about preaching the gospel for charge, or in other words being a paid minister. He says that he did not want to receive earthly payment for his work in the ministry, simply because he didn't want to abuse his power in the word of the Lord."

"Ah," Jamie declared, nodding his head. "So that's where you are taking us."

"Well," Will responded, "it makes sense to me. I mean, it sounds like we need to look for a church that has a lay ministry rather than a paid clergy."

"But," Jamie interjected, apparently frustrated by such a seemingly insignificant point, "today times are different, with the economic conditions totally determining what we eat and how we provide the necessities of life. Everybody I know has to make a living, ministers included!"

"That's a good point, too," Will sighed. "This isn't an easy task, folks, but as your monitor, I think you should put that point on the list, at least to weigh your experiences with different religions."

"That's fine," Jamie confirmed, "but with one qualification. It seems to me that when a minister passes a donation plate, any funds received would at least be partially used to maintain the building, pay the electric bill, and so on. That can hardly be construed as being a paid ministry."

"I think you're right, Jamie," Susan agreed. "And even though I added another point to your list, I want to say something to temper things a little."

"We're listening," Will stated easily.

"All right, here goes. You gentlemen must remember that time has passed since Christ was here, and so, as Joseph says, some things have changed. My mother always said that a person shouldn't throw the baby out with the bath water."

"Meaning?" Will asked.

"Meaning that because something in a church doesn't fit your points exactly, you shouldn't just arbitrarily cast aside the whole religious program. Maybe the true church today *won't* be exactly like the Lord's church anciently."

"It sounds like you should read my notes on the eternal perfection of Christ," Jamie said quietly. "If you did, it might open up —"

"Hey," Will called, interrupting him, "there's the church I told you about, up there on the right."

I nodded, shifted down into second gear, and pulled into the crowded parking lot next to the church.

"All right, lady . . . and gentlemen. This is it."

Jamie straightened his tie, and together the four of us, our hearts pounding with anticipation, walked toward the small but lovely cobblestone chapel.

# CHAPTER
## 9

Frankly, after about ten minutes of that particular service, I found myself fervently hoping that we *hadn't* found the true church. The chapel was beautifully decorated, the minister was young and eloquent, and the people who attended were most attentive. But in spite of all that, the entire affair had the aura of a circus, or at least of a sideshow.

The minister stood at a high pulpit delivering his sermon, while behind him and off to the side, on another platform, a man sat behind a huge and complete set of drums. Surprisingly I knew him, for he came into Anderson Flying 'A' pretty regularly to buy his gasoline. We had visited a little, and I knew that he too was going to college. This, then, had to be *his* way of funding his education. And it was an interesting way indeed.

When the minister wanted to make a point in his sermon, he would pause dramatically and point at my friend behind the drums. Then the drummer would beat out a twenty-to-thirty-second rhythmic cadence. After that sufficient and jarring interlude or underlining, the minister would resume his sermon again, and everyone would begin holding their breath in anticipation of the next dramatic drumroll.

Still, we sat through the service, more I think because we wanted to be polite than for any other reason. At its conclusion, a man passed around a collection plate, and Susan contributed. I would have as well, but payday was not for another two days, and I was as broke as a person could be. Jamie and Will didn't contribute, either, though I never asked them why.

Later, as we were leaving, the minister greeted us at the door and thanked us for attending. We acknowledged his thanks, and then Jamie, with no hesitation whatsoever, asked if he might ask the minister a few questions.

Sounding pleased, the minister readily agreed.

"Sir," Jamie began, "my friends and I are looking at various Christian religions, trying to determine which of them we should join. We have learned certain things about Christ's church as it is described in the Bible, and we are trying to make appropriate comparisons."

"That is a noble task," the minister declared, smiling comfortably.

"Yes, we think so. First, do you make a sufficient living from the contributions you receive?"

The man smiled. "Well, young man, that is very personal, of course, but I will respond in this way. I am not wealthy. But the people respond generously, and my salary is certainly adequate for my needs."

Jamie smiled. "Thank you. I believe that answer is sufficient. My other question concerns your authority. Where did you get your authority to become a minister?"

"From the clouds," the man declared proudly. "I was driving along one day, when there before me the clouds formed a perfect cross. I knew instantly that the Lord was speaking to me, calling me to the ministry."

"Well," Jamie said quietly, "that would have been the impetus, the motivation. And it certainly sounds like it was a tremendous experience for you."

"Oh, I can assure you that it was. I have never seen anything like that in my entire life, nor have I ever been so motivated!"

"I'm certain that you are right. But let me pursue my question, concerning your actual authority. Where, or how, did you receive that?"

The minister looked questioningly at Jamie. "Why," he declared, "I suppose you mean when I graduated from college. At that point I was ordained."

"What college?" Jamie pressed. "And where did they get *their* authority to ordain you?"

"Now see here, young man —"

"Sir, I don't mean to be impertinent. My friends and I are only trying to learn. You see, the Apostle Paul, in Hebrews chapter 5, verse 4, says that no man taketh this honor unto himself, but he that is called of God, *as was Aaron*. As you may recall, Aaron was ordained by Moses, who was a prophet of God. Were you ordained by a prophet? Was there one in residence at your college?"

"No, no I wasn't," the man said quietly. "There are no actual prophets today. Any serious student of religion knows that."

"Do they?" Jamie asked softly.

"They do, I assure you. Now, I am very interested in what you young people are doing. I have thought of Paul's statement often and wondered at it. What other items are you looking for?"

"Well," Jamie replied proudly, "we have compiled a list of fifteen points or evidences —"

"Sixteen," Will interrupted gently.

"No, *seventeen*," Susan prodded. "Remember that Joseph added that last point, about preaching for hire."

"That is right," Jamie said, smiling. "I stand corrected. We have found seventeen evidences in the Bible about Christ's original church organization. For instance, preaching for hire, as Paul described it, seems to be something that did not exist in the ancient church. Another point is that it appears to us as if Christ intended his group of apostles to continue as a functioning organization. Thus we are also seeking a church built upon a foundation of apostles."

"Oh, yes," the man nodded in understanding. "Ephesians. You won't find any such thing in orthodox Christianity, of course. But maybe you won't need to. Have you considered the possibility that we, meaning all modern Christian churches, are built upon the doctrinal foundation those ancient apostles laid out for us? Their writings and teachings are the very foundation upon which *my* church is built, I can tell you that."

"We *have* thought of that," Jamie responded thoughtfully. "Only, we think that Christ intended that group of apostles to continue historically, not just as an idea or a body of teachings. You see, after Judas committed suicide, the eleven remaining apostles met and cast lots to select another apostle, and—"

At that point the minister's secretary interrupted him with news of an important telephone call. Inviting us back at any time to discuss things in greater depth, the man kindly excused himself and was gone.

For a moment we stood, irresolute, and then we walked silently from the church and climbed back into my car.

"True church, huh?" Will teased. "If that drum-rolling nonsense is religion, then I'm thankful to be an atheist."

And of everything that had transpired that night, I felt

worst about what Will had said. I know that Jamie had told Will that neither of us would try to convert him, but I can also say that both of us, secretly, hoped that our experience in seeking out the true church would help Will to see the inaccuracy of his response to his family tragedy.

"What do you expect?" I asked. "It wasn't the exact church we're looking for, anyway. Besides, I know that fellow at the drums. If he's religious, we're all in trouble."

Everyone laughed, and then Will stopped us. "You know," he said quietly, "that really isn't fair. We've got to remember that we can't judge a religion by how good or how bad its individual members are."

"Good point," Susan agreed. "Yet on the other hand, we are told that by their fruits we shall know them. I think we should expect some rather unusual things from the membership of Christ's church, at least as a group."

"Susan's right," Jamie agreed. "In fact, if you will look at my list, you will see that as number eight or nine. I can't remember which."

Our atheist referee and monitor sighed. "It's number nine," he said quietly. "Joe, you're supposed to be the believer, not me. If you would just study Jamie's list . . . "

Susan looked at me with a questioning glance, and I realized that I had forgotten to tell her of Will's atheism and his status in our group. I did so then and she nodded her understanding, and so Jamie continued.

"Thank you, Will. We appreciate your help. So what's next?"

"Er . . . excuse me, gentlemen," Susan interrupted, clearing her throat. "My mind has been spinning since our conversation with that minister a few moments ago."

"It has?" I asked. "But why? The man is a paid minister, so that is one off the list. Then he doesn't claim divine authority, and his church has no apostles or prophets, so that makes three down. What is your mind 'spinning' about?"

"Well, it has to do with what Jamie said in there; the question of the need for there being a prophet alive *today*."

"You mean," Jamie inquired earnestly, "that you don't think there should be one?"

"To the contrary. This seems strange, but I've been thinking about that issue ever since Joseph showed me his list, and I've concluded that if there *wasn't* a prophet alive today, then it would have to be because of one of three reasons."

Well, Susan had our attention, all right. And so we listened with fascination while she articulated her thoughts. And frankly, I was impressed. More and more I was learning to appreciate this woman I was falling in love with.

"First," she declared, "we wouldn't have a prophet today because God has lost His power to call one."

"That couldn't be," I countered. "God is all-powerful, as we've agreed."

"Okay, then the second reason we wouldn't have a prophet is because God doesn't love us anymore. He doesn't care whether we have direction or not."

"What?" Will questioned. "I'm not sure I follow your thinking."

"I believe I do," I interrupted. "The purpose of a prophet is to speak with God, face to face, and to receive God's word for *our* use. Susan is saying that *if* he didn't love us anymore, and didn't want to be involved with us, then he would not provide this vehicle for us to be guided by. Am I right, Susan?"

"Exactly," Susan smiled, her eyes dancing with that mysterious excitement that was hers. "And that leaves just one reason why God would not have a prophet here today. There wouldn't be a prophet because we, meaning the peoples of the earth, don't *need* a prophet at this time."

"That's absurd!" Will blurted unexpectedly. "If there *was* a God, and if he *ever* spoke to his children through prophets, then there has never been a time when his word was needed more than it is today."

I glanced at Jamie, saw him smiling and enjoying the mental gymnastics that Susan had initiated, and so I grinned as well. Susan was great, she really was. I now realized that though her eyes had been my captivators, her mind was going to be my prison. And it would be the most joyful confinement a man could ever imagine. Oh, how I loved her, and as I listened to her reason with my two friends, my love and gratitude for her grew by leaps and bounds.

My mind spinning with thoughts of Susan, I started the engine of my old Dodge relic and began backing out of the parking area of the beautiful cobblestone church.

"Well, gentlemen," Susan asked with a smile, "is my reasoning sound?"

"More than that," Jamie declared. "You have just crystalized what I have been playing with since Joe called about your coming with us tonight. Joe and Will, I propose that we hereby proclaim that Susan Bartholemew be considered, from this moment forward, the official fourth member of our team. All in favor say aye."

The vote was unanimous, and we all congratulated ourselves, though I suppose I was the happiest of all.

"Well," Susan said, once again all business, "where to now? It's still early, and perhaps we can visit another congregation tonight."

"We can go to my Methodist church," I suggested hopefully.

"There's no point in it," Jamie stated flatly. "We *know* it can't be the correct one."

"Oh yeah?" I questioned, feeling suddenly defensive. "And just how do we know that?"

"Because your minister gets paid, too, doesn't he? And I know Methodists don't have prophets leading them."

"Right on both counts," I sighed in resignation.

"I don't think that should matter," Will said. "Jamie, as your monitor, I feel that I should emphasize what Susan was trying to say a little while ago; you shouldn't throw the baby out with the bath water. You guys need to face up to something that I don't think you heard her say. You need to consider the possibility that perhaps *the* church is *not* in existence today."

"What do you mean?"

"I mean that maybe you will have to settle for 'second-best'. In other words, a church that has all seventeen, or even thirteen, of your points, or maybe even just ten of them, may not even exist. Still, a church that contains several of them might. Maybe that is what you will have to settle for."

"I don't think so, Will. Even if a church has sixteen of the seventeen points, it won't be what *I* am looking for."

"Jamie, you gave me the position of monitor. I'm monitoring right now, and you need to listen to me."

Suddenly Jamie broke into a wide grin. "You're right, Will, and thank you. Joe, it is just past eight. How close are we to your church?"

"Fifteen minutes."

"Good. Could we talk to anyone there tonight?"

"Sure. Reverend Walsh is there every night."

"Then, let us be gone."

Precisely fifteen minutes later I maneuvered into the parking lot of my Methodist church. I was nervous, but I was also very excited, for Will's statement had made a lot of sense to me. If there wasn't a *true* church, and personally I didn't see how there could be, then it seemed reasonable that we should seek out a *best* church, one that came the closest to what Christ taught. And, as far as I was concerned, Reverend Walsh ran one of the 'best' churches in the world.

"Reverend Walsh," I said, after we had all been seated in the rectory, "my friends and I have been doing a little studying of religion, and if you wouldn't mind, we'd like to ask you a few questions. My friends know, of course, that you are Methodist, for I have told them so. Beyond that, I thought you would be the best one to answer questions."

"Well, Joe." Reverend Walsh said, smiling easily, "I've never yet entertained a question that I couldn't answer, at least to my own satisfaction."

"Really?" Will asked.

"Absolutely. Of course, most of my answers are composed of just three words — 'I don't know.' "

He laughed, we joined in with him, and I was feeling more at ease by the minute. He really was a fine man.

"Reverend Walsh," Jamie began, "we have gone through much of the Bible and have compiled seventeen points of doctrine, or beliefs, that Christ taught while he was here upon the earth."

"You have? Why, that is wonderful! I had no idea that young college students took such an interest in religious truths."

"I think it's the war," I declared, looking at Susan. "Maybe it's the feeling that life might not be as long as we had hoped."

"I daresay that would do it," Reverend Walsh agreed soberly.

"Concerning these seventeen points," Jamie continued. "I am certain that a more thorough study will bring out even others, but we are of the opinion that if Christ's true church exists on the earth today, these seventeen points of doctrine would have to be a part of it."

"Interesting thesis, young man. Have you considered

the possibility that Jesus organized his church so that it could adapt and grow, therefore changing over the course of centuries to meet the needs of different peoples?"

"We have," Jamie smiled. "However, I personally don't believe that was his intention. If Christ was a perfect being, our very God, as Paul says, then surely he would have foreseen our needs just as he understood the needs of people in his own day. Every evidence I can find points to the idea that he intended his church to continue as he established it."

"Really? Would you mind giving me an example?"

Jamie smiled even more widely, and I sensed for the first time how much he actually enjoyed doing what we were doing.

"Not at all. Jesus chose and ordained twelve apostles. Judas, after the betrayal, committed suicide. That left eleven. But those men, rather than leave it at eleven, or increase it to, say, fifteen because the church was growing, met together and chose *one* new apostle. They cast lots between Matthias and Barnabas. Matthias received the vote and so was brought into the quorum, bringing the number back to exactly what it had been under Christ's mortal ministry — twelve apostles. Then, when another vacancy occurred, Barnabas was brought into the group, again maintaining the number of twelve."

"Hmmm," Reverend Walsh mused. "I do believe you are right, at least historically. But, my friend, things *have* changed. None of the Christian religions have apostles today, so obviously your thesis isn't correct."

"Either that," Jamie agreed softly, "or else none of the churches are correct. But, Reverend Walsh, you have just responded to one of our points, and we thank you."

"And that was?"

"Whether or not you have apostles and prophets in your church."

Reverend Walsh laughed. "Even the idea of that is ludicrous."

"Is it?" Susan asked, surprising me again with her straightforward manner. "I'm not sure it's as ludicrous as it sounds. The Bible says that God is unchanging, from everlasting to everlasting. Why should man have the right to change something that the everlasting God has established?"

Surprised at Susan's logic, Reverend Walsh looked directly at her, his smile gone.

"Young lady, that's a very good point. I'd not thought of it in that manner before."

"Reverend Walsh," Jamie pressed, "we respect the beliefs of the Methodist faith, and so we did not come here to argue or debate. We are simply seeking information so that we can make an intelligent decision. May we ask you a few more questions from our list?"

Reverend Walsh looked kindly toward me and nodded affirmatively.

"Good. Do the Methodists accept the Trinitarian Godhead?"

"We do. *All* Christians do. Is there something on your list about the Trinity?"

Jamie nodded. "There certainly is. In the references to Christ's baptism, the authors of the Gospels refer to three distinct entities in the Godhead. Our research has revealed that the Trinitarian doctrine was manmade, that it didn't even come into existence until some three hundred years after the time of Christ."

"Yes, I know." Reverend Walsh agreed. "That doctrine was formulated at the council of Nice, and then developed more fully in other councils. And you should know that I accept it, too. I have studied it thoroughly, and truthfully

I could not define the Divine Essence any better than they did."

At that point I wanted to ask Reverend Walsh who he pictured in his mind when he prayed, but Jamie was too fast in moving to the next issue, and I never had the opportunity. Still, that elderly, kindly gentleman that the three of us pictured when we prayed was surely something to think about.

"Reverend Walsh," Jamie asked, "where did you receive your authority to preach?"

"From my university."

"And where did they get it?"

"I suppose that it goes all the way back to—"

"The Catholic Church. Am I right?"

Reverend Walsh scowled. "Well, technically, perhaps, but that was a long time ago. I don't think—"

"Reverend Walsh," Jamie interrupted him, "I am Catholic. In all my studies of Catholicism, I never once heard a priest describe how the Catholic Church authorized any Protestant groups to break away. Not recently, not anciently. In fact, when people broke away and formed their own churches, they were, without exception, excommunicated by the Catholic Church."

"Well," Reverend Walsh said easily, "perhaps you are placing more importance on that issue than we do. You see, I believe that all churches can lead us to God, much as all roads lead to Rome. If we bring people to Christ, then I can't imagine that God will scowl and turn them away because they weren't a member of some particular sect."

That sounded good to me, and I nodded at Will, who grinned back. But apparently Jamie did not agree, and neither, to my continued surprise, did Susan. Both of them were shaking their heads.

"I take exception to that, sir," Jamie declared. "And I hope that you don't think we came in here to mock what you believe. I respect that deeply, and I know that Joe does as well. He is a real admirer of yours. But I can better understand my own thinking if I can talk with people like you who are more knowledgable than I am — in other words, if we can agreeably disagree while we explore the reasons why. Does that make sense?"

"It does," Reverend Walsh stated, smiling slightly. "And I promise not to be offended. Please proceed."

"Very well. God is a God of law, and if we have to keep laws, then surely he does as well."

"I don't think God *has* to do anything, my friend."

"But sir, the Bible tells me that he does. Baptism is to cleanse us from sin, and all are commanded to be baptized. Yet Christ, who was without sin, was also baptized, and he told a protesting John that it *had* to be so, in order that the *law* could be fulfilled."

"That is an interesting example."

"Isn't it? Now perhaps you see why I feel impelled to believe that God *lives* laws as well as *gives* laws. That being the case, I think of Paul's statements concerning one Lord, one faith, one baptism, and concerning the fact that God is not the author of confusion. You will readily agree that confusion exists among the various Christian denomina-tions, making it virtually impossible for there to be 'one' of anything. That confusion is what leads me to firmly believe that there must be one true church. God, based upon his own biblical statements, couldn't possibly sanction more than that. Only one, the *true* church, is approved by him, and that church alone holds his authority to act."

Reverend Walsh was quiet, thinking of what Jamie had said. Finally he spoke. "That is a fascinating argument, young man. I understand more clearly, now, why you are seeking apostles. If you are correct, then such men would have to be included in the church, as would some specific form of authority."

"That's right. And that brings up another question. Do you believe in baptism?"

"Certainly. As do all Christians."

"What manner of baptism do you believe in?"

"That depends. If an infant is baptized, he is sprinkled. If an individual is baptized as an adult, he or she has the choice of being sprinkled or immersed. Most people, for obvious reasons, choose sprinkling."

"Why is that?" I asked, intrigued.

"Well, Joe, think about it. If a person is immersed, he or she becomes soaking wet, has to change clothes, and so on. That is terribly inconvenient when a few drops of water will do just as well."

We all nodded our understanding. I hoped that we were through, and then suddenly Jamie was at it again.

"I think it is sad," he said quietly, "that our society has become so convenience-oriented that we arbitrarily change God's laws."

"If I'm not mistaken, young man, your church sprinkles *everyone!*"

"I know," Jamie agreed quietly, "and that is why we are not at *my* church this evening. You see, we are back to the issue of confusion. God is not the author of it, but oh does it exist! Reverend Walsh, may I share with you some things I have learned about baptism?"

Reverend Walsh nodded agreeably, and so Jamie took off with his knowledge and flew, once again surprising each of us present.

"The Synoptic Gospels, Matthew, Mark and Luke, all use the word *baptize* when describing Christ's baptism. And all of them say that he went down into the water, was baptized, and then came straightway out of the water. In other words, and I don't mean this facetiously, he went to the bother of getting all wet.

"To further illustrate, the New Testament was originally written in Coinae Greek, the common or street-language Greek. That was because almost all of the people at the time of Christ spoke Greek and Aramaic, and it was written so that they could read it. In other words, the Gospels were written to promote the faith among the people who might read them.

"In that common Greek, the word baptism is rendered *baptiso*. It is the *only* word for baptism in all of the New Testament, and it means to dunk or to immerse. Interestingly, the word for sprinkling does not appear at all in the New Testament.

"So where did sprinkling originate, you might ask? From a bishop named Cyprian, who presided in Carthage, North Africa, from A.D. 248 to A.D. 258. According to all I can learn about him, Cyprian stood in power next to Rome and was considered a very religious man. Thus, Cyprian was the voice of God in the area over which he presided.

"Now, Cyprian had a friend, a heretic named Novatus, who was sly in all his ways. He wanted to put off baptism until just before his death so that he would have time to work in all of the sinning and riot-filled living that he could. However, he wasn't totally hedonistic; he was also concerned that he might get baptized and then *accidentally* commit a sin that would nullify his baptism. So he kept putting it off, wanting to be certain that his own end was near.

"The trouble was that he was suddenly taken ill and was almost instantly too weak to go down into the water to be baptized. However, Bishop Cyprian told him not to worry. Cyprian then declared that it didn't make any difference *how* a person was baptized; that it was, after all, his, Cyprian's, authority that made it count. So Novatus was sprinkled with a little water, and the idea caught on. As you say, sir, doing it Christ's way is very inconvenient."

"I have heard of Novatian . . . "

"You have? He wasn't the same man, but surely you are referring to the Novatian movement, which flourished from about A.D. 250 to perhaps as late as the sixth century after Christ. That was a protestant movement, even *then*; a puritan revolution against both the Catholic and Arian branches of the Christian faith. The Novatians believed that the church had become depraved, filled with unbelievers and infidels who used it for their own selfish ends. Thus, Novatian, following his excommunication by Bishop Cornelius, founded his own church and had himself elected bishop. But the point is this. To get into Novatian's church, the old baptisms were thrown out, and the converts had to be rebaptized, *by immersion.* You see, Novatian was trying to get back to the old, *true* doctrines — just as we are this evening."

For a moment Reverend Walsh stared at the floor. Then he looked up and, with a sigh and a sincere smile, spoke.

"My young friends, years ago when I was also very young, I set out on a similar search. It led me to my present ministry because I could find nowhere else to go; in other words, this was the very best that I could find.

"But what you are telling me now strikes at the very heart of all I have lived for. I accept that, though, because I have never claimed perfection for my beliefs. I truly wish that everything could be as you have pointed out. I ache to be in Christ's literal kingdom. But with my limited abilities I have not found it, and now I am too old and too committed to begin the search anew. You are very intelligent, though, and very young. Perhaps you will succeed where I have failed. And if for no other reason than to humor me, I would appreciate very much learning what you ultimately find.

"Joe," he said, turning to me, "would you come back and tell me if your quest ever bears valid fruit?"

"I will, sir. Susan and I will come back and tell you."

Reverend Walsh smiled. "I wondered if something was going on between the two of you. Susan, you seem like a lovely young woman. If you're really interested in Joe, you need to know that he'll require a great deal of love and tenderness."

Reverend Walsh winked broadly, and I grinned in embarrassment.

"Actually, Susan," he said gently, "he's a fine young man, and I have great hopes for him. Who knows? If you stick with him, he may even become the great surgeon he aspires to be."

"Thank you," Susan said with a smile. "I fully intend to do just that."

Will and Jamie grinned, and we arose and shook hands. Silently we filed out of the rectory, and I couldn't have felt better. Maybe the Methodist Church didn't qualify in all points, but I would never find a finer friend than Reverend Walsh, and I knew it.

# CHAPTER
## 10

The next two weeks were a whirlwind for me, and it is difficult to remember very much about them. But what I do remember consists of two major issues — Susan, and Jamie's quest. In fact, Susan and I may be the only couple in history who fell in love and then did most of their dating visiting different churches. But then, with less than a week until my departure for Fort Ord, she and I sat alone one evening, contemplating.

"Joseph," she asked as her eyes searched mine, "what are we going to do about the list?"

"I don't know. What do you mean?"

"I mean after you're gone. Are we still going to work on it? Are we still going to look for Christ's church?"

"I don't know. I . . . I've been so busy the last few days that I haven't really thought about it."

"Well, I have. And I think we ought to keep looking."

I grinned at her persistence. "I'll go along with that. It will be difficult though, Susan. I hear that basic training is pretty time-consuming."

"Well, Joseph, if you do what you can, and if you encourage me, then I'll do the same for you. That way whatever we find, we'll be finding it together."

"Sounds great. Now, what about tomorrow night? Are we going to have any togethering then?"

"Oh, Joseph," Susan groaned. "I *can't*. I've got that dreaded lab exam, and I won't be finished until after ten, I'm sure."

"Can I see you then?"

Susan giggled. "We'll just have to see."

Later on I drove Susan home, and for the rest of the night I worried about how lonely I was going to be the following night without her. I needn't have worried though, for Jamie had other plans.

"I know you have no time," he said the following after-noon as the two of us were walking to class. "But I need you there with me, Joe."

"What changed your mind?" I queried. "I thought you had pretty much ruled out the Catholic church."

"I had, Joe, in terms of its being the true religion of Christ. But in fairness to Father Donalew, I sense a need to examine, from our present perspective, the virtues of my faith. After all, it might yet prove to be the *best*, or most accurate, religion on the earth. It is certainly the oldest in Christianity."

"So what do you propose?"

"Just this. I know that tonight is Susan's exam, and that she can't be with you. Will can't break away, either, so that leaves just the two of us. Anyway, I phoned my cousin, Gwen Jackson, who has been acting as scribe to Father Donalew. Seems he has just translated his own version of the Bible and is picking up the completed manuscript at her home tonight."

"And you want me to be your companion in crime to visit with *him*? Jamie, I wouldn't know what to say. I—"

"You really don't have to say anything, Joe. Just be there to give me support. He's as fine a man, and as knowledgable, as anyone I know; and so he should be able to give us some real direction."

"Well," I grinned, "what can I say? You came with me to my church. How can I do less for you?"

"Thanks, Joe. And listen. I don't care what Susan says. I think you're really quite a handsome fellow."

We both laughed, shook hands warmly, and parted. And as we did, I felt a surge of love for Jamie, an emotion that both surprised me and intrigued me. As I said, I'd never had a brother. Had Jamie Deltano somehow filled that vacancy in my life, I wondered? Did I, without planning it, suddenly have a brother, and a sweetheart, too? Both Susan and Jamie had come into my life quite unexpectedly, and I was filled with such deep emotions for each of them that I could hardly comprehend it.

"Pick me up at six o'clock sharp, Jamie," I said, doing my best to lighten up my feelings. "You can treat me to a burger on our way."

"Thanks, Joe. I owe you, so it's a deal. See you tonight."

# CHAPTER
## 11

"Is your cousin married?" I asked, gulping down the last of my fries.

"She *was*. Her husband was killed in a head-on collision a couple of years ago."

"I'm sorry to hear that, Jamie."

"Oh, she's okay now, I think. In fact, she's dating a fellow quite seriously. It's her two daughters, Diane and Donna, that I worry about. They really miss their father."

Moments later, as we wheeled into the Jackson driveway, we were immediately overwhelmed with the attention of the two excited girls. Jamie teased them and played with them for a minute or so, and then Donna, the eldest, grew serious.

"Father Donalew is waiting for you," she whispered. "He says he is in a hurry, but he can take a few minutes to answer your questions."

Glancing over at Jamie, I anxiously sighed my unexplainable reluctance. He merely smiled, winked, and then reached down and scooped both girls into his arms.

"Ladies, this is my friend, Joe. He is a nice man, and I happen to know that he has a package of cherry Lifesavers in his shirt pocket. If you smile nicely, I bet that he'll give you the whole pack!"

Good ol' Jamie, I mused as we walked up the drive. Never misses a trick.

"Hi, Jamie," the woman at the door said. "Please come in. And you must be Joe. I've heard so much about you."

Well, to say that I was taken aback with the charm of Gwen Jackson would be stating it mildly. In the briefest of moments I was welcomed into her home; introduced to her priest, Father Donalew; shown her newly typed manuscript of the 'Donalew Version' of the Bible; and offered a chair.

"You boys must be starved," she exclaimed, handing each of us a large glass of ice water.

"Actually, we just ate," Jamie answered, hesitant to offend his accommodating cousin.

"No matter. I know your weakness, and I've fixed your favorite dessert . . . carrot cake with vanilla frosting!"

With that pronouncement, she was gone, leaving the two of us to our own devices with a seemingly anxious Father Donalew.

"So, Gwen tells me that you boys are experiencing a religious inquiry. Is that right, Jamie?"

"Uh . . . yes, sir," he said hesitantly. "My friend Joe and I are looking into each other's religions so that we can better determine that complex phenomenon called *truth*."

I wondered at Jamie's apparent discomfort with his priest. I had never seen him so much at a loss for words. But then I recalled the night we had spent with Reverend Walsh, and I knew exactly how he must be feeling. This was the man who had baptized Jamie. This was the man who had directed his catechism, had helped him form his values and his understanding of eternal truths. And now, here he was, questioning the very foundations his faith had been built upon. No wonder he was so nervous.

"That's very admirable of both of you," Father Donalew answered. "So tell me about it."

"Uh," Jamie replied, glancing toward me, "perhaps you could explain the Catholic understanding of the Holy Trinity . . . the Godhead."

And so, almost as though he was reading from Jamie's notes, Father Donalew repeated the basic definition as recorded in the Nicene Creed. When he concluded, he smiled warmly in my direction.

There was silence then, and suddenly I realized that Jamie was not going to respond. For some reason he couldn't, and it didn't matter what the reason was. For the moment, at least, Jamie was through with his questions.

And so, feeling pressure to continue the conversation, I cleared my throat and spoke. "Sir, could you please explain where you derive your authority to perform your priestly duties?"

"Surely, son. I have my doctorate of divinity."

"Yes," I agreed, "but who ordained you to your priesthood?"

"A very special bishop, son. You see, the Roman Catholic Church believes in ordination. Mark, who was Peter's scribe, recorded that great apostle's words on the subject, in Mark 3:14-15. Why don't you read it, Joe," Father Donalew instructed, handing me the Bible that had been placed on the table before us.

And so I read these words: "And he *ordained* twelve, that they should be with him, and that he might send them forth to preach. And to have power to heal sicknesses, and to cast out devils."

At his instruction, then, I turned to John 15:16, and read: "Ye have not chosen me, but I have chosen you and *ordained* you, that you should go and bring forth fruit, and that your fruit should remain; that whatsoever ye shall ask of the Father in my name, he may give it to you."

I sat silently, not knowing how to respond. Jamie's church believed in ordination. That was one of the evidences of Christ's true church. And from the look on Jamie's face, he was just as surprised as I was.

"Here you are, Father, straight from my oven!"

I watched our hostess, Gwen Jackson, walking quickly into the room, and I was glad for the interruption. It looked to me like Jamie was going to need to ask the questions, and for some reason he wasn't able to.

When I finished eating, I looked over at my friend and saw that he was still pecking absently at his food. He was either totally disoriented by what we were talking about, or else he was working through something that was far deeper and more troubling than I could imagine.

"Sorry I've missed your conversation," Gwen declared, "but I'm here for good, so please continue."

"Father," Jamie finally spoke, his eyebrows suddenly furrowed with his intensity, "I don't want you to take this question personally, but I have wanted to ask it for some time now. Why aren't popes and cardinals mentioned in the Bible?"

Well, I could have cut the air with a knife, it was so full of instant tension. Looking back on it, I have to hand it to both of them, Jamie and Father Donalew—Jamie for being so bold, and his good priest for being so kind and accommodating in the midst of this most unexpected interrogation.

"Well . . . " Father Donalew began, smiling with a warmth that was truly part of his acknowledged greatness, "actually, Peter was the first pope, even though his title wasn't mentioned at the time."

"Don't you think that is strange, Father?" Jamie inter-jected, honestly questioning. "I mean, Christ placed Peter at the head of his Church just prior to the crucifixion, and yet he didn't give him a title, other than that of apostle. In fact, the title of pope was not given until nearly the end of the eleventh century, when Gregory VIII assumed it. At that time he ordered that it should always remain with the bishop of Rome."

Father Donalew smiled. "I can tell that I taught you well, Jamie. Your research is technically correct. However, it is my impression that the title one assumes is insignificant. The relevant issue is how one serves, and by what authority."

"Of course that must be true," Jamie said quietly. "But I want to pursue this, if you don't mind."

"No, I don't mind."

"Good. Father, what about prophets? According to Paul in his letter to the Ephesians, each of the apostles were also prophets, in that they walked and talked with the Lord and then recorded his word for us in our day. Paul even said that apostles and prophets were the foundation of his church. Father, why don't we use the term *prophet* in re-ferring to the church leaders today? And why don't we call the pope a prophet? Is it because he really isn't?"

Father Donalew did not respond, and so Jamie continued his searching questions.

"And if the pope isn't a prophet, Father, then that brings us full circle to Joe's question of ordination and authority. Paul tells us that no man takes the honor of God's authority unto himself, but that he must be called of God as was Aaron. You certainly remember that Moses, God's holy prophet, took Aaron aside, laid his hands upon his head, and ordained him to authority. And Amos 3:7 says that God won't do anything except through prophets. Father, if the pope isn't a prophet, then how could he possibly give bishops authority to ordain good men such as yourself?"

In the stretched-taut silence of the room, the four of us sat without moving. The little girls, out in the kitchen, giggled over something; we all noted it, and nothing else moved. Finally, with a sigh, Father Donalew shifted position and looked at Jamie.

"Young man, do you understand what you are questioning? Do you comprehend the centuries of good works performed by the blessed saints and martyrs that you are calling into doubt? Do you further realize the jeopardy in which you are placing your own eternal soul, a soul made blessed when you were baptized as a baby?"

Slowly Jamie nodded. "I do, Father. But that brings up another question. Would you please explain your rationale for baptizing newborn infants?"

"Quite simply," Father Donalew answered rather brusquely, "it is done to remove the original curse of Adam."

"Er . . . " I stammered, "could you please rephrase what you just said, sir?"

"It's just this simple, my boy," he said, turning to me. "Adam's partaking of the forbidden fruit became what we call 'the original sin.' All babies are born into that sin. Should they die, to keep them from going into a state of limbo, or natural happiness, without the supernatural vision of God, baptism is performed at the earliest possible moment."

"Let me ask you another question, Father," Jamie interrupted. "It may sound silly to ask, but why did Christ suffer in Gethsemene and then die on the cross?"

"To merit, or to pay, for our sins. You know that, Jamie."

"Yes, I remember well the lesson you gave on that subject. But is that *all?* Didn't you teach me that by suffering and then being resurrected, and thus providing the sacrament of eternal life, Christ overcame, or *paid*, for Adam's original transgression?"

"Hmmm. I see what you mean, Jamie. And what you're really saying is—if that is true, then infants don't really have a curse to remove. Right?"

"Precisely."

"Well, that's one of the mysteries, Jamie. But my personal motto is 'better safe than sorry,' and I suppose that's where the Church stands, as well. To be quite frank, I would recommend the same motto for you."

Jamie didn't respond, and Father Donalew seemed perplexed. He didn't say anything else, but the look in his eyes was one of deep concern. I think that he was aching for Jamie, but of course that is something I will never know. Once or twice he started to speak, but each time he closed his mouth and said nothing. Finally, he simply stood up.

"If you'll excuse me, boys," he said, "I must be running along. Good luck with your quest for truth. I wish all young men had the same thirst for heavenly light and knowledge that you have."

Shaking our hands, and gathering up his finished manuscript, Father Donalew thanked Gwen for her work, bid her a kindly farewell, and was gone.

For some time, then, she and Jamie and I reflected upon the events that had transpired. Father Donalew had been very willing to discuss his beliefs, but not as willing to hear ours. Yet it seemed evident that he feared for the welfare of Jamie's questioning soul. Why hadn't he said more? Why hadn't he put forth a greater effort in Jamie's behalf?

That really bothered Jamie, and I could tell from his silence that he was still evaluating it, trying to understand his priest's reactions.

"I don't really know what you're going to find on this search of yours," Gwen said as we went out her door a little later, "but if you ever learn the answers to all of your questions, please let me know."

"We will," we both chorused as we climbed into the car. "We surely will."

# CHAPTER
## 12

Not until the following Sunday morning, the day before my departure for Fort Ord, were Jamie and I able to get together with Will and Susan for a de-briefing of our experience with Father Donalew. Finished with that, Jamie looked at all of us.

"I know we're about to head out in all directions," he said, summing up the impending sense of loneliness we were each beginning to feel for the others. "But before we go, I have one request."

"I hope it isn't to date Susan," I laughed. "She's already spoken for."

"That's correct," Will said. "I'm the man for the job, and I hereby serve such notice. I promise to take real good care of her for you, Joe."

"Why, thank you, Will," I answered. "That's very kind. And I trust you, too—about as far as I can throw you!"

We all laughed, as did Susan, and I was about to carry things a little further when Jamie brought us all back to order.

"Enough is enough, you guys," Jamie said wisely. "Actually, my request is quite simple. It has to do with prayer."

Suddenly Will and I began looking at the floor. Until this moment our experience together had been serious, yet purely with intellectual and social overtones. We had approached our errand from an academic viewpoint, and now Jamie, in one sentence, was suddenly changing all of that.

"Will, I don't want in any way to offend you, but I want us to pray for each other — for our safety and well-being, as well as for our continued focus on this unexpectedly complex quest that we've begun."

Again, as he had successfully done so many times before, Jamie Deltano had reached deep within himself and exposed even more of who he truly was.

"I think your request deserves a reply from me," Will responded, clearing his throat. "I . . . uh . . . I want each of you to know, including you, Susan, that this experience has meant a great deal to me. I must admit that I am still not standing in your Christian, believing shoes; but I feel better about myself, and about . . . my desire to continue searching. . . . For if there is a God, and oh how I wish that there might be, I know I will need him before I cash in my chips."

"Spoken well," Jamie replied, smiling. "You're a fine man, Will, and I will always appreciate your honesty and friendship."

That set the stage for what happened next, as each of us, in turn, shared our feelings of love for each other, and our gratitude that we had been able to spend our college year together.

"Now," Jamie said when we had finished, "what about that prayer?"

It was strange, but as badly as I wanted to, I just couldn't bring myself to offer a vocal prayer. At least I couldn't bring myself to go first.

"All right," Jamie said quietly. "That's fine. But if you wouldn't mind kneeling with me, I'd like to pray for all of us."

Slowly we all dropped to our knees. And then, as if it was something that he did every day of his life, Jamie began talking with the Lord. It wasn't even a prayer, either. At least it wasn't like any prayer I had ever heard. Jamie just talked, as if he was talking with me, and I found myself wondering if maybe God had entered the room and was standing in front of Jamie, listening.

I looked but could see nothing, and then I lost myself in what Jamie was saying as he prayed for each of us by name, and I forgot to even wonder any more. For some reason, as Jamie prayed, I felt out of breath, almost as if I was choking. I also got incredibly warm, in a way I had never felt before. But even more than that, I felt a sense of belonging, a strange and beautiful closeness to the Lord that I had never known before.

Later that evening, as Susan and I pulled to the curb in front of my apartment, I felt like I wanted to cry. To hide my emotions and to prolong our last evening together, I invited Susan in for a late snack.

"Make yourself comfortable," I said, grinning and pulling her close to me. "I'm going to cook this one."

"Do I dare eat it?"

"Hey, babe, I've been cooking my own meals for six years. In fact, we're going to have steak."

"Steak? At this time of night?"

"Well, leftover steak. Just turn on the radio and I'll have this ready in no time."

While Susan examined the huge blackboard that was now filled with Jamie's scribbled notes, I sliced some leftover New York strip sirloin into thin pieces and fried them in a hot skillet. While I watched the pieces sizzle and curl, I thought for perhaps the millionth time of Susan, picturing her face the way it had been that first night in the gas station—soft, pleasant, lovely. Now I was always looking past that, at the beauty of her soul and her mind. Of course, I still noticed her beauty; believe me, I did. But my thoughts no longer stopped there, and even now I find that a very difficult thing to explain. However, I think it translates into actual love, the kind of love that grows deeper with each passing day and week and month and year. And I did love Susan, more than I had ever imagined that I could love anyone.

Would she enjoy being married to me, I wondered? Was I the kind of a man who could make a woman of her caliber happy? I didn't know, but I certainly knew that she could fill my needs and that I would cherish being married to her.

For a moment then I thought of my mother and wished that I could have known her so that I could compare her strengths with those of Susan. Actually though, all I could remember of my mother was her yelling at me, complaining to me, or demanding from me. I could not think of one single positive memory to cling to.

So I tried to compare that memory with Susan, and the results were so absurd that I burst out laughing.

"What's so funny?" Susan called.

"Nothing. I was just thinking about you."

"Oh, great. You think I'm funny now. . . . "

"Hey, lady, I think you're simply the greatest woman in the world. How am I ever going to keep the men away from you while I'm gone?"

"Not to worry, Joseph. I'm not anywhere near so attractive as you think I am."

"Don't tell me that, or I'll be disappointed. Somehow I've become convinced that you're ravishing."

Instead of answering, Susan stood up and walked to the blackboard.

"Joseph, I didn't know that Jamie had written so many things about the seventeen points."

"He never stops adding, Susan. He's so consumed by our project that he comes in here every day to study the list and to make changes and evaluations."

"Even when you aren't home?"

"Especially when I'm not home. He likes quiet, and with me away, this apartment has it all. What are you looking at . . . what point, I mean?"

"This one that says we will honor Sunday as the Sabbath day."

"Is that a big deal?" I asked.

"It would be if you were Jewish or a member of the Seventh-day Adventist faith. Apparently he's done a lot of studying about it. I assume that these abbreviations are to reference books?"

"I think so."

"It fits. Apparently he's even researched out the origins of the calendar. From what I can make out, his conclusion is that Christ rose on the first day of the week and thus sanctioned it the Lord's day. That ancient first day corresponds exactly with our modern first day, which is Sunday. Hence, Sunday is the Sabbath."

"Jamie is thorough. What's the point next to it?"

"That officers and members of Christ's church will receive continuous revelation and inspiration from God."

"He and I were discussing that one last night. Susan, do you believe that such a thing is possible?"

"I don't know, Joseph. According to the scriptures he has noted here, God promises to reveal his will to mankind. Let's see, this says that he does that through the workings of the Holy Spirit, or through the whisperings or . . . the still, small voice of the Holy Ghost.

"Hmmm," she continued. "Joseph, Jamie concludes that

this revelation or inspiration effects our feelings, or our minds, and that we don't very often actually see or hear things."

I heard that and thought of the overwhelming feelings I had experienced while Jamie had been praying a little earlier. Had that been brought about by the Holy Spirit, I wondered? I didn't know, but I had felt some things I had never before experienced, I did know that.

"Joseph, he also says that members of Christ's church will be payers of tithes and offerings. Then he has here that Webster says a tithe means a tenth, or ten percent. Do you know any churches that require their members to give ten percent?"

"I don't," I said, thinking. "But Susan, why would a church require it's members to pay ten percent when it doesn't pay it's ministers to preach?"

For a moment there was silence. "I don't know, Joseph. That's a very good question. When we find this church, it will definitely be something we'll want to ask them."

"When?" I asked. "Not *if?* You seem pretty definite."

"I am."

"Which," I teased, "pretty, or definite?"

"I'm definite, Joseph. I *know* the Lord's church has to be here somewhere, and I'm going to look until I find it. Are you going to look with me while you're in the military?"

"Of course. I already told you that. But Susan, I want you to know something."

"What's that, hon?"

"That besides being definite, you're incredibly pretty, too."

Quickly Susan left the blackboard and walked to me.

"You know, soldier boy," she whispered, putting her arms around me from behind, "I've never before experienced the feelings that I have for you."

"Ditto."

"Well, aren't you the great romanticist! Joseph, I love being in love. Especially I love being in love with you."

I took a deep breath, for what I wanted to say came hard for me. Still, I had to try, for I might never get another chance. "You s-surely know how to get inside a fellow's heart," I declared stumblingly. "Susan, you have given me so much happiness, and . . . and well, we'll be together again before you can say Jack Spratt."

Turning around, I gathered her into my arms, and while the steak sizzled and cooked, I closed my eyes and felt the encompassing warmth of Susan's love.

"I'm going to miss you something awful," I whispered brokenly.

"I . . . I'll miss you, too, Joseph."

"Will . . . will you wait for me?"

"You know better than to even ask, silly."

"You're right, but I just want to hear you say it."

"You goofy guy," Susan giggled, wiping the tears from her own eyes. "You lovable, goofy guy. Of course I'll wait for you. Just hurry and come back to me, all right?"

I nodded, and once again I buried my face in her hair.

"It's my turn for a request, Joseph," Susan finally whispered, pulling away from me. "This is in addition to all of the rules we've made about letters and phone calls."

"For you, I will walk on hot coals, I will cross the Rocky Mountains on foot in a raging blizzard, I will—"

"You really know how to win my loyalty, don't you, Joseph."

"I . . . I'm trying to learn."

Again there was silence, as we each savored being in the arms of the other. At last, knowing that the hour was late, Susan pecked at my ear and then whispered softly, "My request, Joseph, is that before you take me home tonight, we have prayer again, together."

Well, when Susan said that, I was suddenly filled with the most unusual tingling, just as I had been during Jamie's prayer. It was sort of like warm bells, except that there was no sound. I just tingled all over, and I knew without a doubt that what Susan was requesting was right.

"That does it," I declared. "Now I know we're meant for each other. I was thinking exactly the same thing a little while ago."

"You were?"

"Yeah. Back at Jamie's. I was really touched by his prayer, and I found myself wishing that I could find a way to have an experience like that with just the two of us."

"Well, you might have asked, Joseph."

"I know. It's just that I . . . I've never prayed out loud before, Susan. Yet I know we must learn to do it if we're going to have the kind of home and family that I think we both want."

"Joseph, dear, is that a proposal?"

"I . . . I guess I haven't been very official about it, have I?"

"Not hardly. But I'm waiting. . . . "

"All right, all right. Nag, nag, nag!"

"Joseph . . . "

I grinned and dropped to one knee. "Miss Susan Bartholomew, will you agree to spend the rest of your mortal days with the greatest leftovers cook in L.A.?"

"I'd *love* to!"

I arose, tenderly we kissed, and afterward we took each other's hands in our own, bowed our heads in prayer, and had the most beautiful moment imaginable. Together we committed ourselves to our Maker, entrusting our future, and our lives together, into his hands.

And neither one of us even noticed that our sirloin strips had burned to a crisp. Or cared, either, for that matter.

# PART FOUR

May 26, 1942
to
October 23, 1942

# CHAPTER
# 13

When I left for Fort Ord, I carried in my wallet the list of seventeen points that had been compiled by Jamie Deltano, and I carried in my heart the promise given me by Susan Bartholomew — that she would wait for me and marry me. Those, as it turned out, were to be my greatest treasures in life, and my greatest sources of comfort.

The war, what little we heard of it, was turning out to be costly and frightening. Along the Atlantic coast a dim-out was in effect, hopefully stopping possible attacks from German submarines. In the South Pacific, the Battle of the Coral Sea had been fought, and we had lost the carrier *Lexington* and nearly lost the *Yorktown*. Yet our planes had inflicted heavy damage on the Japanese, and so the marginal victory was deemed America's. But on Corregidor, General Jonathan Wainwright, who had been captured by the Japanese, had broadcast his surrender of American forces, and had encouraged all U.S. forces in the Phillipines to surrender. It was neither a happy nor a hopeful time, and so the atmosphere, when I entered Fort Ord, was intense.

Basic training, as everyone knows who has experienced it, is an eight-week ordeal that one has to go through to understand. It is an uninterrupted chain of days and nights composed of total regimentation — too little sleep, terrible food, and physical and emotional abuse. Yet I endured, because I had no choice, and because I could gather strength from the almost daily letters from Susan.

Also supporting me were the letters from my friends. With the exception of one serious letter from Will that I received during my first week in basic training, both he and Jamie wrote crazy, zany epistles — and both joked regularly about Jamie's continuing quest. They reported visit after visit to various churches, and truthfully they must have become involved in some tough and eye-opening conversations. Or at least Jamie called them that. Will called them arguments, and he told me that they occasionally got pretty hot and heavy.

Jamie hadn't been back to his Catholic faith, but in one letter he told me that he had had another conversation with Father Donalew, where he had discussed, quite openly, four more of his points or evidences.

They were, first, that the members of Christ's church would experience miracles, including divine healing, being first anointed by the elders with holy oil and then prayed over.

His second point of discussion concerned the sacrament of the Lord's supper. He emphasized that the sacrament *represented* the body and blood of Christ, but did not actually become the body and blood. This point made much sense to me, since I had never understood how the doctrine of transubstantiation was supposed to work anyway. But apparently he and Father Donalew had had a difficult conversation over it.

The third point they discussed was that Christ's church

would expect and eagerly anticipate the resurrected Lord's second coming, when he would appear in the clouds, in glory, sometime in the "last days." That issue also produced some heated conflict.

His fourth and final point of discussion with Father Donalew was that members of Christ's church would be persecuted for their beliefs. As I thought about it, that point didn't seem particularly fair. But on that point, at least, Jamie and his priest had agreed. Father Donalew had described the martyrs down through the centuries, Jamie had told him of his own research into some of their lives, and the two had parted friends, knowing that in at least one area of Jamie's search, they agreed.

Susan had also had an experience with a minister, and I did some deep thinking about what she wrote. Jamie had determined that Christ's church would build temples, beautiful buildings that would be built for unique purposes and ordinances. They would contain a place called the "Holy of Holies," and only certain people would be allowed to use them.

Susan wrote that she had read about Solomon's Temple, and of course there had been a temple during Jesus' life, from which he had driven the moneychangers both at the beginning and at the end of his three-year ministry, giving fairly obvious evidence that he thought temples ought to be sacred places.

But as for modern times, she had seen a Masonic Temple once that was reserved for the use of Masons only, but which was, to the best of her knowledge, more social than religious in nature. She didn't think that would qualify. Beyond that, she wrote that she had never heard of any other Christian churches that had temples.

Armed with what little information she had had, she had gone through the telephone book and had found a church that worshipped in what they termed a temple. She had gone there, and apparently her experience would have been funny if it hadn't been so frightening. She didn't tell me any details, but I gathered that as far as she was concerned, the activities participated in that temple were neither sacred nor divine.

I laughed at her account and wrote an immediate letter telling her to stop searching alone, and to go only if she was with either Will or Jamie. I grinned as I thought of the green light I was giving my friends to go out with Susan, but I had absolute confidence in them all, and to be truthful I never did worry about it.

So I stored my friends' experiences in my mind and did my best to concentrate on, and survive, basic training.

When it finally ended eight weeks later and graduation ceremonies were held, I was thrilled to see Jamie and Susan seated together in the stands. Will had joined the Air Force and was in his own basic training, and I missed him. But dressing right and parading past both my best friend and my sweetheart, was a joyful, tearful moment for me. There they were, the two people who meant more to me than anything else — honoring me as I completed basic training.

The following two days were glorious in every way. We feasted in the restaurants of Carmel and laughed and played on its glamorous beaches. But like all other good things, it had to end. And it did, just as my civilian life had ended some weeks before, with Susan and I again in each other's arms, our eyes filled with the sorrowful tears of separation.

"I don't know if I have the strength to continue without you," she whispered, the diesel engine of my Greyhound chugging and rattling nearby.

"Sure you do," I replied, not nearly as confident as the words sounded.

"I love you, Joseph, and I'm so proud of what you're doing."

"Couldn't do it without you, Susan. I love you, too, more and more each day."

"I . . . I can't wait for us to be together."

"Me neither. Maybe we ought to set a date, so we can plan toward it."

Susan looked up at me, and new tears swam in her eyes. "Joseph, that would be wonderful. I wish we could do it right now!"

"Me too," I grinned. "But let's look at Christmas. I should be through with all my training by then, so I shouldn't have any trouble getting leave."

"But what if . . . if you get shipped out?"

"If I do, babe, they'll give me a leave before I go, and we can tie the knot then. Sound fair?"

"Oh, Joseph, I don't know if I can stand to wait . . . "

Once again Susan and I were in each other's arms, and I really couldn't imagine anywhere else on earth that I would rather be.

"Hey!" Jamie shouted, "break it up, Joe. You're not going to make it easy on me during the ride home. I'll be dishing out tissues to Susan the whole way back to L.A."

Susan and I wiped away tears, laughed, exchanged embraces, and wiped away more tears. Then, before I knew it, I was rolling along toward the train that would take me to my next base.

Two long days later I found myself unpacking my duffle bag in my new barracks at Fort Sam Houston, Texas. There, in the rolling hills near San Antonio, I would train to be a medic.

The days passed quickly, and although I was lonely for Susan and for my friends, I found the medical field to be interesting. Actually, I found myself thriving on it, and no matter how many hours I put in, I somehow felt that if I could just give it a few more, then I would learn the rest of what I needed to know.

It was there, of course, that I determined to apply for Officers Candidate School in anticipation of becoming a doctor of medicine. Susan was thrilled, and she squealed with excitement when I called and told her of my decision. She then asked if I had prayed about it, which I was soon to learn had become her predictable response to life. Always she turned to prayer, and she developed a reliance upon God that is difficult to describe.

Anyway, I hadn't prayed, but for her sake I did so. Nothing miraculous happened, but I felt good about having prayed, and when I applied, my papers went through like a breeze.

Finished with medic training, I was sent to Fort Benning, Georgia, to O.C.S., and then to jump school. I successfully completed them both, eight weeks each, and found my life taking on proportions that, until just a few months previously, I had not thought possible.

Susan took the train out twice that summer, and with each weekend together we found ourselves more in love than ever. But besides being in love, both of us were still working on our great quest. On both weekends together we randomly selected and attended nearby church services. The first church we attended was Unitarian, and we were especially impressed with the spirit of love among its members.

In our brief discussion with the minister afterward, Susan boldly brought up another of Jamie's points, one that I didn't understand at all, and questioned the man about it. Jamie had determined that if people died who had not been baptized, that members of Christ's church would have authority to vicariously perform that sacrament for them. He called this "baptism for the dead" and used Paul's statement in 1 Corinthians 15:29 to show that it had occurred.

The minister had never heard of such a thing, but as I listened to Susan's logic, it certainly seemed to answer some of the nagging questions I had had about the gospel being made available to all people.

"I don't understand it, Susan," I said later as we walked across the post to her bus stop. "How does a dead person get baptized?"

"I'm not sure, honey, but Jamie says that it doesn't mean that corpses get baptized. He says that the phrasing 'for the dead' implies proxy work, a living person standing in for another who has died."

"Seems like a lot of work."

"I'll say. More than I can imagine, at least right now."

"Have you ever found a church that does that?" I asked.

"I certainly haven't. In fact, Joseph, I'm having a difficult time finding churches who believe in, or even understand, more than three or four of Jamie's points."

"Yeah," I agreed, "me too. I still haven't found one that has apostles and prophets. But I'm looking!"

Susan smiled and kissed me. "So am I, darling. I'll be back in another six weeks. Until then, I love you."

I watched her bus drive away and was filled with an unaccountable sense of sorrow and loneliness. It wasn't just that I was already missing Susan. It was . . . well, I hardly knew. I just had an impending feeling of doom, and for the entire six weeks until Susan returned, I couldn't seem to shake it.

During her next visit, we left the post on Saturday and attended the Seventh Day Adventists church. In my opinion, Jamie had clearly established that the Sabbath Day was to be Sunday. But Susan, always more open-minded and accepting than I was, convinced me that we ought to at least attend their services.

We did, and I found them very impressive, with the people exhibiting a strength and oneness that they seemed to derive from their genuine concern for each other.

I remember too that there was a convenience market next to their chapel, and I had a peculiar feeling as I read the sign that hung above the entrance: CLOSED ON THE SABBATH — OPEN ON SUNDAY.

As we visited later, both Susan and I realized that we were finding it increasingly impressive to see the good, religious peoples of the world — those who kept the commandments and sought to live by the Bible as they best understood it.

"Susan," I said as we sat on the lawn just outside the base, "I know that God loves all those people. He has to, the way they try to live such good lives. It hardly seems fair to have just one true church."

Susan smiled. "It doesn't to me either, Joseph. However, I'm certain that my feelings come from my lack of understanding, for I know that God is just in all ways. All his children, no matter their faith, will be treated fairly. I know that.

"I know, too, from studying our list, that there *is* a single, true church that belongs to Christ. Everyone must seek that church out and unite himself or herself to it. Joseph, have you thought any more about which church it might be?"

Slowly I rolled over until I was lying on my back, staring up. Then I reached out and took Susan's hand.

"I think about it all the time, Susan. I just don't know anything."

"Are you praying?"

"Yes, off and on."

"Joseph . . . "

I grinned. "Actually, more on than off. It's just that I don't think God has answered me."

Susan sighed. "He hasn't answered me either, except to give me a wonderfully good feeling every time I ask him if we should continue pursuing our list."

"You get *that?*"

"I do, Joseph. I feel as if I am going to melt, or explode in my chest, or something like that. It is an amazing feeling, and I think it must be the Holy Spirit."

Now I looked at her. "You're serious, aren't you."

"I am."

"You know, I get a funny feeling sometimes, too." I got that far, and then for some reason I couldn't let down and go any further. I wanted to tell Susan about my occasional tingling feelings when I prayed, and I wanted just as badly to tell her about the gloomy feelings I had been having. But I couldn't do it. For some reason the words just wouldn't come out.

"Yes, Joseph? When do you get your funny feelings?"

"Oh," I said seriously, "like when I haven't eaten for several hours . . . "

"Oh, Joseph . . . "

I grinned to hide my emotional pain and sat up. "But I'll tell you what, oh beauteous one. Your train departs in an hour or so, and I don't want you to leave until we can pray together. The base chapel is right over there, and I imagine it is a fairly private place. Shall we spend our last few minutes alone in there?"

Susan was surprised, and it showed. "In a church? Praying? That's where, and how, you want to say good-bye?"

Standing up, I took her hand. "What's wrong with churches?" I asked casually as I lifted her to her feet. "I like churches. I've spent a lot of time in them lately. And as far as saying good-bye goes, I read in the Bible just the other day about 'holy kisses'. Aren't those the kind that occur in churches?"

Susan giggled like a little girl, and that afternoon we had a sweet time planning our Christmas wedding and saying good-bye within the solitude of the base chapel.

# CHAPTER
## 14

Apparently the army's intention had been that I would work as a medic with the paratroopers overseas, but somehow that never materialized. Instead, I stayed in Fort Benning, teaching safety to the officers and enlisted men who were training to be paratroopers.

Although I was quite busy as a new second lieutenant, I still kept up my search. Jamie and Susan did also, and they wrote me regularly about their adventures. I also got several letters from Will, and I could see a change in his thinking. More and more he was asking me the 'what if' types of questions, and not doubting so much, as he had always done before. I asked him once why he was asking me instead of Jamie, and he wrote back that Jamie had little patience with answering his letters. So I wrote him regularly and then forwarded his letters to Susan.

Some two or three weeks after Susan had returned home from her second visit, I happened to be in town on a Sunday pass. I was with a man named Rence Paxman, who, since O.C.S., had become my closest military friend.

"Joe," he said as we walked along the street, "I don't understand you. Every weekend you announce that you are going to attend some church or other, and yet never have I heard you mention the same one twice. Don't you ever plan on settling down and attending a specific church?"

I looked at him in surprise, for in spite of the tremendous religious tumult I continued to feel within me, neither of us had ever spoken a word about religion.

"Why? Would you like to suggest one?"

Rence shook his head. "I don't have a church, Joe. I saw my mother's meager financial resources bled dry by phony radio evangelists who never did a thing but call across the airwaves for her to send them money. I guess that soured me on churches."

"I've wondered about those people," I said. "Some of their preachers give dandy sermons."

"Yes, they do that, all right. But it's like Paul said, and like Mother finally realized and told me. Outwardly they wear sheep's clothing, but inwardly they are ravening wolves. 'Touch the radio dial and you'll be saved,' they say. Or, 'Hold your hand on the radio and you will be healed. And oh, yes, dear flock, send your money so that God will see your faith and reward you.'

"Mother had so much faith in the Lord, and every week she would send in her few dollars to those guys. But her rheumatoid arthritis never got better, she couldn't have been any closer to Jesus than she already was, and those radio preachers simply bought big cars and built hundred-thousand-dollar houses with the money that she and millions of other poor, righteous people sent them. I tell you, Joe, that's a real racket they run.

"In fact, I'll tell you another scripture Mother told me those guys were fulfilling. She told me this after she had figured out their pitch and had learned through prayer that you can't buy your way into heaven, which they had been encouraging her to do.

"Paul says, to Timothy, I think, that in the last days perilous times will come when men will be lovers of their own selves, covetous, boasters, proud, blasphemers, and so on. They will not endure sound doctrine, but after their own lusts shall heap to themselves teachers, having itching ears."

"Your mother says they do that?" I questioned.

"I'll say. One says you don't need to be baptized, another says you do. One says that a relationship between unmarried people is adultery, another says it's natural and beautiful. I could go on, but there isn't any point in it. The whole thing, no matter how you shake it out, comes down to this: most of those airwave evangelists have itching ears and are heaping to themselves teachers after their own selfish lusts."

"That's pretty final, Rence."

My friend grinned. "Don't get me wrong, Joe. I believe in religion and in God, but I don't know where to find him. And I don't think those radio guys know any more than I do."

"Well, neither do I know where to find him," I said with a sigh. "But a buddy of mine got me looking into different religions, and ever since then I haven't been able to stop."

"Gee, that sounds crazy. In spite of those radio guys, I always sort of wanted a church. But . . . well, I don't know. Nothing ever seemed quite right."

"Would you like to go with me today?" I asked. "I mean, it probably won't fit either one of us, but like I said, I promised."

Rence grinned. "Fit? Like a shirt?"

"Sort of."

"Yeah, Joe, maybe I'd like that. You know, I'll tell you

something funny. For about two weeks now I've felt like I ought to go to church. I don't understand it, but that's what I'm feeling. It's sort of like God is whispering to me, telling me to get to know him. You know what I mean?"

I grinned awkwardly, feeling suddenly invigorated. It was almost as if this was Jamie Deltano I was talking to, or maybe even Susan.

"I'll say I know! Listen, Rence. Let's look for a church and go in. Right now."

Rence's eyes lit up like a neon sign. We slapped each others' backs and started walking, and as though it were destined to be, right around the next corner we found a church.

"What do you know," Rence said in awe, "just like a blooming miracle."

I was a little surprised myself, especially since it turned out that the services were about to begin. The church was called the Church of Christ, which I had heard of but knew nothing about. We went inside, sat down near the back, and took part in the service.

"Brothers and sisters," the minister began, breaking into a smile, "tonight I would like to use as my text the words of that great apostle Paul, which he wrote to the saints in Ephesus. In Ephesians chapter 2, verses 19 and 20, Paul says, and I quote, 'Now therefore ye are no more strangers and foreigners, but fellow citizens with the saints, and of the household of God; and are built upon the foundation of apostles and prophets, Jesus Christ himself being the chief corner stone.' "

Well, when the man said that, I started to shake like I had the chills and fever. I was buzzing all over my body, and truthfully I became embarrassed, fearing what people would think if they happened to look at me.

"Now," the man continued, "I know we don't have

apostles and prophets in our church today, even though it would be a great blessing to have such gifted men as Paul leading us. But I am thankful to have the promptings of the Holy Spirit in speaking to you this evening, and I pray that they will remain with me.

"I have been thinking about this for some time, brothers and sisters, and I believe that we are in a time of reformation. That is, we are gathering truth and conducting ourselves as best we can—in preparation for the *fullness* of the gospel to be restored to the earth."

As the minister spoke, my mind reeled in continued recognition—for he was saying some of the same things that our group had concluded almost a year before. In fact, one of Jamie's strongest points was that there had to be a restoration of some sort in Christ's church in the latter days. And now here this man was speaking of the same thing.

"After much study," he continued, "I have written several tenets that I believe Christ's church would have if it were to be here with us, in its fullness, today."

Suddenly, listening to him, I found my eyes welling up with tears. He was where I was! We were all in exactly the same place! Almost without thinking I reached into my pocket, retrieved a small notepad that I always carried, and began to record his words.

"First," he continued, smiling in our direction, "our Savior's church would have a great missionary program. It would consume the earth, simply because it would also have his power, or his priesthood, within it. Those missionaries would declare the message of the gospel to every creature.

"Second, members of his church would perform miracles daily. In addition, this church would have an effective and fulfilling women's organization and an equally fulfilling teenage and small children's organization, thus reaching the needs of each and every member.

"If Christ's church were on the earth today, it would have the same organization that existed in the primitive Church. It would not be a 'one-day-a-week' religion, but would permeate our lives seven days a week.

"Now, before I expound upon these tenets of a complete church, I would like to say that there is one final trait that, I believe, would exist in the Master's church. Again Paul spoke of it, as he said that he would preach the gospel without charge, that he abuse not his power in the gospel. This is difficult for me to say, especially since Marjorie and I are dependent upon your offerings. But when Christ's church is here in its fullness or completeness, there should not exist a paid ministry—but rather a lay ministry should swell its ranks."

"Yeah!" Rence whispered loudly as he poked me.

I looked at my friend, nodded, and turned back to listen to the minister. But by then my heart was about to burst. In every detail, this man's conclusions seemed in total agreement with Jamie's points and the conclusions of Rence's mother. In essence, he had begun the same list that I had, in its complete form, in my hand, and I was so excited that I could hardly sit still.

Afterward the minister, who was an elderly man, came up and shook our hands.

"Young men," he said, "I'm glad that you came to our service. I imagine life in the military gets a bit lonely."

We both nodded.

"I'm glad we came, too," Rence declared. "I enjoyed your sermon. Except for the money part, I didn't know any of those things about Jesus and his church."

"You don't believe that money should be paid to ministers and churches?" the man asked.

"Oh, no," Rence declared, "it isn't that. I just think there must be some 'right' way to do it. I wish I knew what it was."

"So do I," the minister said sadly. "But I find, after all these years, that I know very little. In fact, young man, I have concluded that all I do know is that I *don't* know much about God's correct church."

"But *I* know a little!" I declared excitedly, feeling more enthusiastic than I could imagine. "I have a list too, much like your own, except that it is somewhat longer."

"A list?" the man asked. "But I don't . . . "

"Let me show it to you, sir. Last year some friends and I began to examine the Bible, looking for things that would exist in Christ's church if it were here today. My list has seventeen points on it, and you discussed five of them tonight."

"May I see your list?"

"Sure. It's pretty messy and crowded, and I don't have any of the scriptural references that my friend Jamie found. But you're welcome to look at it."

The minister took it, and with pursed lips he read it over carefully.

"My goodness," he said when he had finished, "that *is* a list. Are you certain that they are all correct?"

I smiled. "Reverend, I'm not certain of anything. But I think they are, and so do the others who have been compiling this with me."

"Well, well, well. I see you reject Trinitarianism. I do also, though it is more because of a feeling than anything else. And let's see, you also accept the need for apostles and prophets, you accept the second coming as literal, and you expect members to pay tithes and offerings—yet you ask the clergy to preach for free. Does that make sense to you, young man?"

"Not really, unless God uses his money for something other than supporting his ministers. My friend and I have been talking about that today, and such a conclusion sort of makes sense. But I don't know, sir. It's only a guess."

"Well, your guess makes sense, and it happens to be the conclusion I too have reached. However, I *don't* know exactly how such money would be used. Let me see . . . what is this about two books of scripture that will be used in the last days?"

"Uh . . . I hope I can remember. I think that's mentioned in the Old Testament, where somebody talks about joining two sticks or scrolls or books together into one volume."

The man looked up, his eyes wide with understanding. "Ah, yes! The sticks of Joseph and Judah that become one. I have often considered that scriptural reference but have never thought of it as meaning that two books of scripture would come forth."

"I don't know, sir. I remember my friend saying that the stick of Judah had obvious reference to the Bible, which was a history of the Jewish nation. Whatever the stick of Joseph had reference to, he didn't know. And as I said, neither do I."

"Well, that is an interesting theory. Hmmm. You believe in the virgin birth, as do I, and in a literal heaven and a literal hell. Yet you think that there will be many rewards after we die?"

"Yes, sir. Paul says that there are many glories in the resurrection, all as diverse as the sun, the moon, and the many stars. I think he means rewards."

"Interesting. I hadn't . . . My goodness, this is an intriguing idea. Do you really believe that there is such a doctrine as baptism for the dead? I mean, I know that Paul mentions such a thing, but do you actually think that he meant it?"

"I . . . I think so."

"But *why?* Why would such a thing be necessary?"

I took a deep breath, for I felt that I was treading on

some very thin ice. "Well, if Jesus really meant it when he said that all people had to be baptized, then I think the answer to your question is obvious."

"And that is?" the elderly man asked.

"That those who have died without the chance for baptism will yet be allowed the privilege."

For the next ten minutes we discussed the issue, taking opposing sides, and neither of us convinced the other. Yet the man was amiable, and I felt a great closeness to him as we came back, time and again, to the issue of a restoration that would occur within the church. Of course, neither of us understood exactly what that meant, but we agreed that, should it happen, we would likely recognize it.

"And you, young man," he said, turning at last to Rence, "are you the silent partner in this search?"

"No, sir. I . . . I didn't know anything about it, at least until this afternoon. I don't know anything much about religion, either, except what my mother taught me."

"Then . . . you must not have attended much church in your life."

"That's right, I haven't."

There was a brief pause, and then Rence turned to face the gentle minister. "Sir, lately I've been thinking that I ought to get to know the Lord. Do *you* know him?"

"Know him?" the reverend repeated quietly. "I think so. I mean, I know him as well as a man can come to know him from studying about him. I have never seen him, of course, or talked to him. But occasionally I have felt his Holy Spirit when I've prayed, and so in that sense I know him, too. Young man, do you suppose that he is giving you these feelings you are having so that you will study? And pray?"

"Study? You mean read the Bible?"

"Of course."

"I tried once, but it didn't make much sense."

The minister and I both smiled.

"It takes time, son. I've been studying the Bible for years, and I still have many questions. You can tell that from our discussion of a few moments ago."

"If you still have questions," Rence pressed, "how can you know the Lord? Can't he give you the answers you seek?"

"Rence," I said, "it isn't quite like that, not anymore."

"Your friend is right, son. I wish that it wasn't so, but in our day the heavens seem closed. God has revealed his word, and except for allowing us to feel the Holy Spirit upon occasion to encourage us, he has left it up to us to come to grips with the meaning of his words. Some days, though, I wish he *would* speak again."

"Well, if God won't speak to me," Rence muttered, "how can I get to know him? How can I get in touch with him?"

"You pray," the minister declared quickly.

"But why should I pray if he isn't going to talk to me? That seems sort of crazy to me."

Sadly the man shook his head. "So many of you soldiers are without understanding. If you had faith, you would know that God doesn't always answer — sometimes he needs only to hear. That should be enough for any of us."

"But I have so many questions. How can I get them answered? How can I find out what I'm doing here? Who am I, really? What or who am I supposed to be? If I die, where am I going to go? Reverend, I don't know if I even care about all those ancient people who lived in Bible times. I'm mostly concerned about me, right now, today. I want answers so badly, and I don't know how to get them."

"Then you're like all the rest of us, son. None of us have those answers, and we won't until the restoration comes that Paul spoke of. That's why we need to walk through this life by faith. One of these days, though, when Paul's restoration takes place, there will be prophets and apostles here again, and we will have the word of God revealed to us continually."

"I'm sorry," Rence said, shaking his head. "I don't think that I can bear to wait, to not *know* . . . "

"Uh . . . sir," I interrupted, wanting to somehow lessen the discomfort Rence was experiencing, "I just want to thank you for . . . uh, for what you said tonight. I don't think you'll ever know how your words affected me."

"Why, thank you, son. I'm not always a very good man, at least yet, but I really do study the scriptures with my heart turned toward heaven."

"I know you must sir. I know you must."

"If I gave you my card, would you mind making and sending me a copy of that list of yours? I would very much like to have it, and the scriptural references, if you have them available. Would you do that for me?"

I smiled. "The list is easy. If I can find all those references, then I'll send them, too."

"Thank you," the man said, smiling gently. "And God bless both of you in this great quest you have undertaken."

We shook hands, Rence and I returned to the base in silence, and I found myself thinking all the way back about Jamie Deltano.

Good grief! Did everyone alive have the same unanswerable questions? I was starting to think that they did, and more and more I was convinced that I either had to push my closeness to the Lord until I found him, or acknowledge that he truly wasn't there.

*Was* God really there, I questioned? And if he was, why did he allow so much confusion about him to reign? It didn't make much sense to me, and I said as much to Rence.

"I don't get it either, Joe. You'd sure think the answers would be more obvious than they are."

I nodded in agreement. "You want to talk, Rence?"

For a moment he thought about it. "No," he finally said, "I don't think so, Joe. Maybe I'll go try another crack at my Bible."

"Good idea. Give me a call if you want to discuss what you read."

Rence considered that thoughtfully. "I appreciate that, Joe. But I think maybe I need to be alone, just me and God. Maybe that minister is wrong. Maybe God *will* answer me. I sure hope that he does. Maybe he'll even tell me where I'm supposed to be going."

"I hope so, too," I said as we stood together in the darkness. "I'd like to hear from him too."

We made plans to get together the next night so that I could share my list with him, and I watched as he walked away into the warm darkness of the night. My heart ached for him, and again I was oppressed with my feeling of despair. Would he find God, I wondered? Would he find Christ, and peace?

Would any of us find those things?

# CHAPTER
# 15

The next morning I was in the middle of some paperwork when word came back that a jumper had forgotten to snap his chute to the plane. It hadn't opened, and he had fallen to his death.

As medical officer on duty, I went to the site—and to my horror found that the dead man was my friend Rence Paxman!

"Sheesh," one of the other medics whispered. "What do you think happened?"

"He forgot to hook up to the plane," another said quietly. "Look! You can see that the cord never even got pulled."

"I'll bet that was a long twelve hundred feet."

"Oh, wow. He'd for sure have known it was coming."

"He did," I said quietly. "Maybe for a long time before today."

"You mean he did this a-purpose?"

I looked scornfully at the man, wiping away the tears in my eyes as I spoke. "Anyone who says that didn't know Rence Paxman," I declared.

"Joe, I didn't mean—"

"I know. What I meant was . . . for days, maybe weeks, he has had a feeling—something about a need to get to know God, and to find out why he was alive."

"Why?"

"Yeah, *why*. I couldn't tell him, though. I don't even know why I'm alive. It's like there is this giant eternal mystery, and I'm living right in the middle of it. So was Rence."

"I guess maybe we all are."

I looked at the man. "I guess so. At least now Rence might be learning some answers. I hope he is."

As I helped the others carry Rence's shattered body back to the base, my mind was whirling. Was it possible that God had been trying to get through to Rence, maybe to warn him? Or to prepare him, possibly? *Something* had surely been turning my friend's mind toward religious things. But if that was the case, then the heavens *weren't* closed at all. God was still there, trying to get through to us. And maybe he couldn't because no one was listening anymore. I didn't really know, but for the next few weeks I was a mighty sober young man. And with each passing day, I found myself turning more and more to the Bible.

On the morning after Rence's death, a new platoon of jump-school recruits arrived, and I was assigned as advisor to one of the squads. Looking back, I remember that they hadn't been there even a day when I sensed that there was something different about them, something unusual. But it was several days before I began to realize what it was.

Jump school started out with forced runs, which always lasted for one hour. On the first day the men ran for one minute, walked the next, ran the next, and so on until the hour was over. On the second day they ran two minutes, walked one, ran two minutes more, walked another one, and so on. The third day the running increased to three minutes, and it continued to increase until the troops were running for the entire hour.

This forced run was a grueling ordeal, and every day a few men dropped out of it. That meant that the dropouts didn't have to run anymore, but it also meant that they were instantly assigned to the infantry and shipped overseas. That knowledge alone had kept many running during training, including me.

But as I watched them, the thing I began to notice about the new squad was that the running didn't seem to bother them. They did it; they either grumbled or laughed about it, depending upon conditions; they helped others to survive by carrying their packs in addition to their own gear; and they seemed to thrive on what they were doing.

The squad consisted of very rough men, at least physically. They beat each other with their fists, they were always shoving and tackling each other and scuffling about, and yet I never heard one of them profane or grow angry with the others. Their jostling was always strictly in fun.

There were other noticeable differences, too. The squad ate together in the officers' mess, and the cook was soon complaining that they drank a disproportionate amount of milk and juice. They also ate a lot. Not one of them smoked, and one day I realized that I had never heard any of them tell any of the numerous raunchy stories that were constantly circulating about the post.

I wondered about these things, and I wondered too that their barracks was always the most quiet after lights out. Those men seemed to actually enjoy keeping the rules.

Suspecting that they had been together all their lives and had pulled some strings to stay together now, I was surprised to find that they were from many different places, mostly out West. Two or three were from California, like me, and the rest were from Arizona, Colorado, Nevada, Idaho, Utah, and Montana, with one lone man coming from Kansas.

So, I didn't understand them—yet neither did I ignore them. They were such fine men and soldiers that I, and most of the other officers as well, developed a keen respect for them. I found myself hanging around them when I could, and we all became at least speaking acquaintances.

Then one morning we were up at twelve hundred feet, heading for our drop-zone. I found myself standing next to Steve Weisenburger, a big, strapping farm kid from Idaho who seemed to be the undisputed leader of the group.

"Isn't this great?" he shouted through the noise of the prop blast.

"Great?" I asked back, wondering if maybe he had slipped a cog.

"Yeah! Look down there, how pretty that is, with the sun clearing out the morning mists. In Idaho you don't see trees like this, and I love 'em. I love the soil here, too. If we had this rich soil back in Idaho, we could grow anything. Of course, we would also need the water . . . " Suddenly he grinned. "What we need in Idaho is this whole blasted state, leaving out just the humidity and the mosquitoes. That, I think, would do the trick."

"You'd take the chiggers, would you?" I teased.

"Oops," Steve chuckled. "Forgot them. Leave out the little beasties, too. I don't know if my legs will *ever* heal."

For another moment we stood together while I examined the man's face. He was actually excited about the jump, and he was so wrapped up in what he was seeing and feeling that I don't think he even remembered I was there.

"Aren't you a little afraid, Steve?" I asked, bringing him back to the present.

"Afraid? Not at all. Should I be?"

"Oh . . . I guess not. Jumping scares me to death, though. I'm glad I'm just running this tub instead of going over the side with the rest of you. I never want to do that again!"

Steve squinted out the door, his clothing rippling in the prop blast. "What's to be scared of, Lieutenant?"

I stared at the man, amazed. "Of dying, that's what! One of my best friends was killed just before you guys arrived. That scared me, and I have yet to recover. Maybe I never will."

"Yeah, we heard about that. It's too bad, too. That's enough to make anybody sober up. But you know, Lieutenant, a fellow shouldn't be scared, even of dying. To my way of thinking, dying can't be all that bad. It might hurt a little at first, but death itself wouldn't be bad. I think it would be kind of nice to be back with Heavenly Father."

"And you wouldn't mind that? There's nothing here that you'd miss?"

Steve grinned. "Well, not exactly. Don't get me wrong. I like living, and I intend to keep on doing it for as long as I can. In fact, I have a sweetheart back home, a gorgeous woman named Mary Lou French, whom I can hardly wait to spend a long, long life with. When I think about living with her, I'd just as soon *never* grow old and die. But if I can't avoid death, and no one I know has ever made it out of this life alive, well, then, why shouldn't I prepare for it and just expect that it will come and get me one day."

"Waiting without fear?"

"Waiting with excitement is more what I mean."

I looked at him, and I don't know why I should have been surprised, but again I was. He certainly seemed like a calm son-of-a-gun.

"How can you say that?" I asked, shaking my head. "I don't understand you guys."

"Lieutenant, it'll be like my first jump, like a new adventure. I think I know what I'll find there, so the only unknown is the manner of getting through it. That's more to be anticipated than feared."

Steve was suddenly busy then, hooking up for the jump. Then he checked each of the eleven others in his squad and turned back to me.

"Lieutenant," he said as he waited for the jump light, "it seems to me that if a man can't answer three simple questions, then in a great measure he will waste his entire life. And he'll have real reason to fear leaving it."

At that instant the green light came on. Captain Weisenburger smiled cheerfully, and a second later he was out the door and gone, the first in a string of twelve billowing puffballs of nylon parachute, all heading with so much ease for the drop-zone.

All the way back to the base I sat in that empty airplane, thinking, wondering. What three questions was he referring to? Was I wasting my life because I didn't know them? And I didn't know them, either. I had absolutely no idea what Weisenburger had been talking about. But sitting in the noisy solitude of that aircraft, I made up my mind that I was going to find out. And, by golly, I was going to do it that very night!

# CHAPTER
## 16

H ey, Lieutenant, how're you doing?"
Steve Weisenburger's booming voice was ample warning for the eleven other men, who, as I looked at them, were instantly polishing their boots. That was a great military pastime, polishing boots. Every night the boots were polished, and every day the shine was totally destroyed. But that was no deterrent at all. It just meant that the shine had to be done better the next time. And on these men's shoes it usually was.

"Captain Weisenburger, can we talk?"

"Sure. Pull up a bunk and have a seat."

The men grinned, for the absence of chairs was a constant complaint among the men, especially since they were now officers.

For a few moments we talked about the weather, about Idaho, about farming, about the bugs in the latrine, and so on. And finally, as I felt certain all twelve had known that I would, I brought up the issue of those questions.

"You said today, just as you jumped, that a man would

waste his life if he didn't know the answers to three questions. I'm afraid that you threw me. I don't even *know* the three questions, let alone the answers."

Steve smiled. "Sir, the questions are easy. They are, *Where did we come from? Why are we here?* And, *Where are we going?*"

For an instant I thought he was teasing about the post, and I almost reacted. But then I realized that he was asking questions of a far more serious nature, the exact questions my friend Rence Paxman had asked the night before he had died — and again my heart felt like it was about to leap from my chest.

"Do you mean," I asked, "where did we come from *before we were born?* Is that the question you are asking?"

"Exactly."

"Nobody knows that," I said quickly, almost scornfully. And I did not miss the quick smiles that appeared on the faces of the group of boot-polishers who surrounded me.

"Don't they, Lieutenant? Surely, to questions as important as those, somewhere there must be answers."

"And now you men are going to tell me that you have them? The answers, I mean?"

Steve grinned. "We don't have the answers to everything, but we certainly do have answers to those three particular questions."

I laughed, but not because I thought anything was funny. I was suddenly very nervous, and I'm not certain why that was. Maybe I thought I had run into a nest of religious fanatics, though I ought to have known better than that. But I did think it, I remember. I also remember feeling nervous because I was so afraid that they might *not* know. I mean, what if they didn't? What if they were as wrong as everyone else I had spoken with throughout my life, including the clergymen I had been listening to and questioning for the past several months.

Why, even Susan had had no luck in finding the church that matched the list we had compiled, and I for one was starting to get discouraged.

"Well," I finally said when I had stopped chuckling, "are you going to tell me the answers to those questions or not?"

"Probably not," Steve said as he lay back on the bunk.

"Why not?"

"Because I don't think you're ready to hear them. But I'll tell you what, Lieutenant Altman. If you'll answer some questions of my own in an honest manner, we'll see where it takes us."

"What do you mean, 'honest manner,' " I growled, upset that he had seen so clearly through me. "I'm always honest."

"Good. Then we should have no trouble. Tell me first of all: do you believe in God?"

"Absolutely. And it's my goal each day to learn a little more about him."

"All right ." Steve grinned, sitting up. "Here's a question *about* him. Do you think that God plays favorites among his children?"

I looked at the man, and in my mind was the conversation Susan, Jamie, Will and I had had our first night out together.

"I think," I said, masking my emotions, "that if he's the sort of God I've been learning about, then he surely doesn't play favorites."

"You're right. He doesn't. Now, Lieutenant, do you believe in the Bible?"

I smiled. "Want to take a look at how mine has been worn down? I'm not the best example of living its teachings, but I surely am getting acquainted with it."

"Good! Can you accept the fact that the Bible is a history of God's dealings with the people in the area known as Palestine?"

That question threw me, and so I thought about it. But the more I thought, the more sense it made. In fact, I began to tingle as I realized that his question might be related to Jamie's idea that the Bible was the stick, or book, of Judah or the Jews.

"Yes, I think I can accept that," I said, hiding my mounting excitement.

"All right, can you accept that fact that Jesus Christ was sent here, by God, to organize his church?"

Now I really tingled. Something unusual was definitely going on, and I was determined to find out what it was.

"If you only knew how many times that question has crossed my mind this past year, and how many scriptures I've found to support it, then you probably wouldn't waste time asking. But absolutely, *yes*, I am convinced that Jesus formed a church. The trouble is, it was back in his day and not now, and that is a tragedy."

The men quickly looked at each other, but this time there were no smiles or behind-the-hand chuckles. Now they were as serious as I was, and I felt that we might finally be getting somewhere.

"That's a good point, Lieutenant. Sounds a lot like playing favorites, doesn't it."

"Yes. In a way it surely does."

"All right, let's make it even harder. Can you accept the fact that the American continents, both north and south, were populated in the days of the Lord Jesus Christ?"

"Not hardly," I chuckled. "That's plain crazy."

"Is it?" Steve asked quietly. "Jared, you've been studying archaeology at Arizona State. Tell this good officer what you've learned."

A quiet man, seated on the bunk across the aisle, looked up from his gleaming boots.

"Sir, haven't you ever heard of the ruins in Central and

South America? There are a lot of them, ruins of dwellings and entire cities, and temples and pyramids that are even larger and more ornate than those in Egypt. National Geographic has done a lot of work in excavation, and many of their issues have featured these ruins. Haven't you really ever heard of them?"

"Well, I . . . I guess I have — if that's what you're talking about."

"It is. These ruins are standing today, evidence of massive civilizations of people who lived, grew old, and died, for thousands of years before Columbus ever stumbled upon our shores."

"But those are the Indians!"

Steve grew serious. "That's right, Lieutenant. And aren't the Indians *people?*"

Instantly I realized how silly I had sounded, and my face turned beet red. "I guess that was pretty stupid, wasn't it. It's obvious that there were people in the Americas when Christ was in Palestine."

"You're right," Steve declared. "It is obvious. But now, think of this. Can you accept the fact that the Father, who loves *all* his children, would send his Son to a group of people who lived in a place roughly the size of the area between Los Angeles and San Diego, and about fifty miles wide, over in Palestine, and at the same time turn his back on the millions of his children who lived in the Americas?"

Slowly I shook my head. "No, that doesn't seem right to me. And I know a few others who have been bothered by that, as well."

"Well, Lieutenant, as a matter of fact, God *didn't* turn his back on the people here, or anywhere else, for that matter. Do you believe in Christ's crucifixion and literal resurrection?"

"I do. There is a lot of evidence for that in the Bible."

"Again, you're right. And in the midst of that evidence is a thought-provoking statement. May I read it to you from your Bible?"

Almost buoyantly I reached into my pocket and pulled out my copy of the New Testament, which I had brought along because of a feeling that our conversation would turn to things religious.

"This scriptural declaration of Jesus Christ is found in the tenth chapter of John, verses 14 through 16. It says: 'I am the good shepherd, and know my sheep, and am known of mine. As the Father knoweth me, even so know I the Father: and I lay down my life for the sheep.

" 'And other sheep I have, which are not of this fold: them also I must bring, and they shall hear my voice; and there shall be one fold, and one shepherd.'

"Lieutenant, who do you think the Lord means when he uses the term *sheep?*"

"He means the people — *us.*"

"That's correct. He means all the children of God. Now he says here that he has sheep where he is, who know his voice. But he also says that he has sheep in another fold, another location, who must also hear his voice. The result of that will be that all the folds or locations of God's children will become as one."

Well, when Steve Weisenburger made that declaration, it was as if a million bells went off within my brain. The sensation was so profound that I couldn't even hear what the man said after that. I do know that he told me something about being able to show me the records of that other fold, but I was so caught up in what he had already said that I didn't listen. I not only didn't, I couldn't!

These men, who by now were all crowded around me, nodding with each of my correct answers, had certainly jarred me. I knew they had just given me further evidence of Susan's seventeenth point, made the night we had visited Reverend Walsh and my Methodist church. That point was that the true church would be able to explain the apparent inconsistencies in who had, and who did not have, access to Christ's church. And it would further be able to show why the others did not need it, or, if they did need it, how they would all be able to receive it.

Of course, that was where Jamie's point concerning baptism for dead people came in. I had come to that conclusion already and accepted it. But until that moment I had never even thought of the possibility that Jesus Christ might have visited people other than in Palestine.

But now these men, with their questions and scripture quoting, had shown me that Christ himself had stated that all people had to hear his word, and that he had even gone to declare it to them.

The very idea of this staggered me so thoroughly that I was left speechless. I stared at them as I tried to formulate a question or two, and in the silence that followed, a piercing whistle sounded an air-raid drill.

"Oh, no!" I groaned as I rose to my feet. "I want to continue this, Weisenburger!"

"So do we," he shouted as he headed for the door. "How about tomorrow?"

I nodded, knowing that at last I was going to learn something that might aid our great quest. The trouble is that knowing and learning are sometimes whole worlds apart.

# PART FIVE

October 24, 1942
to
December 6, 1942

# CHAPTER
# 17

A t mail-call the next morning, the word was out that the battle on Guadalcanal Island was going badly, and that we had lost at least one and maybe two more carriers, *Hornet* and possibly *Enterprise* in the Battle of Santa Cruz. There was also the rumor that Allied forces under Eisenhower were going into North Africa against the Germans, and that we needed to be ready to ship out. And finally, I received a short note from Jamie, and his news was the most tragic of all. Our friend Will Huckstedder had been killed in a plane crash somewhere in the South Pacific.

Numbed with grief, I walked slowly toward my assigned aircraft. Will Huckstedder, the one among us who I thought might be least prepared to go, but who had been making such an earnest effort, was suddenly dead. No longer was he able to seek for himself. Now he was truly on his own quest, gone to . . . gone to . . .

But I didn't know *where* he had gone. Just as with Rence, I didn't know where Will had gone either. What if they had gone nowhere? What if life was really as Will had once described it in one of his letters: just a big crapshoot, which, once it was over, was over!

Oh, wouldn't it be wonderful to *know!* If only somebody really did. Why, news of that nature would be worth all the wealth a man might accumulate throughout his life.

I suppose what happened then was my fault. I know that I was totally oblivious to what was going on around me. I was so caught up in Will's death, and in my own deep fears and concerns, that I didn't even hear the taxiing aircraft. All I know is that suddenly it was there, bearing down on me, the whirling props a dim, almost invisible blur of destruction.

For a fraction of an instant I froze. And then my reflexes, conditioned and trained to a fine point, took over. With a twisting lunge I threw myself off to the side, and in that fraction of a second when the twelve-foot prop chewed through the very space where my body had been, in fact *was*, I saw my own instantaneous and horrible death.

Only I didn't die. I had moved just enough that the whirling prop didn't chew me to pieces. Instead, the tips of the blades caught at my still-twisting, still-falling-away shoulder. I felt what seemed like a solid whump against my back, and the next thing I knew I was lying on the asphalt, the darkness of the plane hovering above me.

I tried to get up but couldn't, and only then did I see the great amount of blood beneath me and realize that it was my own. I rolled over and felt for the first time the pain, hot and red and somehow heavy. Then the pain faded, and I seemed to be away somewhere, drifting along without a care in the world.

The next thing I knew, I was in an ambulance, listening to a medic bark orders. I started to get up but felt another red wall of pain wash over me, and then I was in the hospital, in pretty bad condition.

I was there for six weeks, much of the time not even aware of my surroundings, giving the bones and tissue a chance to knit themselves back together. Only, for some unexplainable reason, that knitting didn't occur, and I became somewhat of a medical problem.

Weisenburger and his buddies came to see me twice, as I remember; but I couldn't talk to them because of my heavy medication. Then they were shipped out, and I never did get a chance to ask them any more questions.

Because Susan was the only family that I had, the army flew her out in a military transport. I remember being happy that she was there, and wondering why we hardly said anything to each other. She was with me for a full week, but obviously it was not one of my more lucid ones, so I don't remember much about her visit. I do recall telling her that we were still going to be married in December, and I wondered at her tears. Knowing what I do now, I'm certain that she understood more about my injuries than I did.

I remembered one other thing, too, though it was vague and I didn't even think of it until much later. Susan was sitting beside me one day, reading a book. Finally she put it down, reached out, and carressed my arm.

"What's wrong?" I asked, concerned at the tears in her eyes.

"Joseph," she answered as she fought to bring her voice under control, "I think I may have found it."

"Found what?" I mumbled.

"Our church, Joseph. What we've all been seeking for so long. The true church of Jesus Christ. So far, my darling, it fits all the points that we have compiled."

"That's just great," I mumbled groggily. "Maybe we can tell Will and Rence . . . "

I started to say something else, but I guess I went to

sleep, because that was the end of my memory. When I next awakened, it was to see Susan standing above me. She was crying, and I remember wondering if she always cried. Then I realized that she was telling me good-bye and saying that she would see me for Christmas. I couldn't understand why she was leaving so quickly, and it was some time before I learned that she had indeed been at my side for an entire week. But she had, she was already leaving, and I could hardly remember anything we had talked about.

For the remainder of that six weeks my body stumbled along the recovery path, making very little progress. There was a great deal of infection, a couple of emergency surgeries, and so much pain that many times I found myself envying Will and Rence. It would have been wonderful to know that my pain was over and that I could slip into death and just sleep forever.

The trouble was, I really didn't want to die, at least yet. I would not go until I had found the true church! I wouldn't, and day after day as I lay trying to recover, my most-repeated prayer was that I be allowed to live long enough to conclude what had become my personal quest. Only I received no answers, and I didn't get any better. Instead I simply clung to life, and the military was forced to deal with me.

On December 4, when I had given up all hope of getting back to California in time for Christmas, or maybe even *ever*, I was suddenly transferred to a hospital in Santa Barbara, just a few miles from Susan's home.

I was taken west in a transport plane, and though the journey was not long, it was not good, either. I don't know how it happened, but as the medics were wheeling my gurney down the ramp out of the plane, something caused the wheels under my head to collapse. I slammed into the ramp on my head and shoulders and felt a terrible stab of pain as though someone had ripped my entire shoulder and arm away from my body. The next thing I knew, I was again in an emergency ward, with Susan sitting beside me.

"Joseph!" she whispered, "Joseph, can you hear me?"

Weakly I nodded that I could.

"Sweetheart," she asked through her tears, "are you all right?"

"I am . . . now that you're with me."

"I have been, for almost two days. It's December 6 already. How did you ever get them to send you *here?*"

"I'm friends with all the generals in Washington," I grunted, grinning weakly. "How's my girl?"

"Now that you're here, Joseph, I couldn't possibly be better."

"That's . . . what I like to hear."

For a moment there was an awkward silence. Then Susan took my hand, and I could see her forcing a smile.

"At least you're not late for our wedding," she said, doing her best to sound happy.

"Yeah, I guess . . . maybe not."

"What . . . what do you mean?"

"Susan," I grunted weakly, "I . . . I've had enough experience to know . . . when things don't look good. They don't look very good for me."

Tears welled into Susan's beautiful eyes, and I did my best to smile. "But don't you worry, Babe. I . . . I'm not going . . . to cash in my chips until I . . . find that true church . . ."

"Do you still . . . believe those things on that list?"

I looked up at her, aware of the catch, the hesitation in her voice. She sounded almost afraid, though I couldn't imagine why that would be so.

"I've *got* to," I answered honestly. "I've spent the last year looking, though, and I haven't found it. But if I'm . . . dying, then I won't go until I know . . ."

"You're not dying!"

"Susan . . . "

"You can't, Joseph. You just can't!"

Slowly I reached out and took her hand. "I won't, Susan, at least not until I find that church. That is if it exists."

"It exists, darling! It says right in the Bible that God is unchangeable."

I grinned. "Isn't that . . . the point you came up with that first night we went out shopping for religion?"

"Yes it is," Susan said. "That was the night I started to find my husband . . . and my church."

"Started - to - find - your *church?*" I repeated very slowly. "Susan, what are you saying?"

Susan smiled and took my hand in both of hers. "Joseph, I told you back at Fort Benning that I thought I might have found the church we've been looking for."

"You did?"

"Yes, there in the hospital. We even had a little discussion about it. However, as I remember, you didn't say much."

I thought back, and for the first time that particular memory returned. It was hazy, but it was there, and I wondered that it had slipped so far into my subconscious thinking.

"I . . . think I remember. No details, though. Just that you thought you might have found . . . something."

"Well," and in her excitement Susan squeezed my hand, "now I am certain of it."

"Are you serious?"

"Yes, I am. About it, and about marrying you! That's why I know that you aren't going to die."

I grinned. "My goodness. I've . . . I've never seen you so certain. Wh-where is this 'true' church?"

"It's all over the world, Joseph. Here and there, wherever a few people are gathered together in the name of Jesus Christ."

"And what is it called?" I asked, almost afraid to hear her response.

"Are you ready for this? It's called The Church of Jesus Christ . . . "

That warning bell was ringing suddenly in my mind, and I could clearly see Jamie writing on the board that Christ's church would likely be called by his full name.

" . . . of Latter-day Saints."

I coughed, not really because I had to cough, but because I had to do *something*. "The Church of Jesus Christ of Latter-day Saints?" I asked, trying to understand what was happening to me. "Isn't that kind of a long and funny name?"

"Yes . . . and no," Susan smiled. "They're called that to distinguish them from the saints in former days."

"I thought the Catholics were the only ones who believed in saints. I thought that was why Jamie put it on our list."

"Then you *do* remember it being there?"

I did my best to nod. "I . . . remember it. 'Worker saints', he called them. I just can't imagine that there are many people on this earth who are that righteous."

Susan laughed. "That isn't what it means. Any person who is a member is called a saint. I'm sure they have people in the church who are wicked, though I hope not as many as there are people who are good."

"In other words, people in this church are just ordinary people?"

"Well," Susan hedged, "I think so. I've only met two of them, and they seem wonderfully ordinary to me. I . . . I haven't ever visited their congregation."

I twisted to get more comfortable in the bed but found that it did little good. Whatever had happened in that fall, it had been serious. I could hardly move, and even lifting my arm took a major effort. Besides, my mind felt like it was flowing in and out, and—

Suddenly I knew. I *was* dying. It was no longer just a maybe that had to be worried about. Now with the reinjury of my shoulder it was a certainty, like Susan's love or Jamie's quest. And just as suddenly I knew that I couldn't let down, couldn't stop breathing until I knew God and his church! I had to keep pressing, keep asking questions, until I knew!

Oh, if only I had Jamie back with me to help—

"Why haven't you gone to their services?" I asked, my voice weak with exertion and pain.

"Joseph, are you all right?"

"Yeah, I . . . I think so. Why haven't you gone?"

"I didn't want to go until you were with me. This is something that you and I must do together, discover together. Joseph, you remember once I told you that I thought a religious man would make a better husband and father? Well, I still feel the same way. And you're one of the finest, most religious men I've ever known. That's partly why I love you so much. For us both to stay that way, we've got to do this hand in hand."

"Susan," I said with a sigh, trying to keep my eyes open, "I don't like to say this, but I . . . I don't think we will be doing *anything* hand in hand anymore . . . "

"Joseph, you keep saying that, and I keep telling you— you are going to be fine! According to Elders Sharp and Carlson, God can heal anybody, even a stubborn army officer."

Again the warning bells! Jamie *had* written that Christ's church would believe in divine healing. Did that mean that anybody could be healed? I didn't know, but I was certainly having funny feelings about it all.

"Elders who?" I asked, trying to concentrate on something other than my pain.

"Sharp and Carlson. They are the two who have been telling me about the church."

"How do you know these old men are right?"

Now Susan really giggled. "Old *men?* They're not old, Joseph."

"But . . . but you just said they were elders."

"I know I did. But that's a title, Honey. Remember, Jamie wrote it down under the heading of 'same offices'? These men are both in their early twenties, but they are called elders because that is their office in the priesthood."

"Priesthood," I declared, starting to sit up. And then I gasped with the pain that struck my shoulder. "Aaaagh!"

"Joseph . . . "

"It . . . it's okay. It's just when I move wrong. I . . . Susan, that priesthood thing is something I heard about in Georgia. Did . . . did we have that on our list?"

"Yes, we did. Maybe you've forgotten. We also called it proper authority, which is the same thing. Elder Carlson says it is man's authority to act in the name of God. They have it, and so do a lot of other elders who are serving, at their own time and expense, to tell people about their church. And if you remember, Jamie said—"

"I know," I said, interrupting her and squinting my eyes against the pain that was climbing up my shoulders. "He said that members would be workers in the true church of Jesus Christ. I suppose that their ministers are unpaid, too. Am . . . am I right?"

"You certainly are. Only they aren't called ministers. They are called bishops, and so on."

I sighed, leaning back. "And these two guys . . . elders have convinced you that they believe all seventeen of our points?"

"They have, Joseph."

"And . . . what about apostles and prophets? I suppose they have them, too?"

I thought I would have her there, but the instant I saw the smile light up her face, the instant I saw the lights dancing again in her eyes, I knew I hadn't.

"They have twelve apostles, Joseph, and their church is directed by a man whom they revere as a prophet of God. I'm telling you, everything fits, just as Jamie said it would."

For a moment or so I was quiet, doing my best to think. Could Susan be right? Was it possible that she had actually *found* Christ's true church? I didn't know, but once again I was filled with that curious tingling—

"Joseph, are you all right?"

"Yeah, I think so. I was just wondering . . . "

"Maybe you shouldn't try so hard. You're as white as a sheet."

"Like I saw a ghost? Maybe I did . . . maybe I did."

"Joseph, once you've met these Mormon fellows, you'll . . . "

Now I turned and really stared at the woman who sat next to me. "Mormons? What are you *talking* about?"

Susan, her face filled with surprise, looked at me.

"Joseph—"

"You said they were the Church of Jesus Christ of saints something or other," I stormed, feeling angry but not clearly understanding why. "You didn't say anything at all about Mormons!"

"But that's their nickname, silly. That's all it is."

"Well," I stormed, "I can tell you with a certainty that I'm not interested. I've heard of the Mormons! They're a weird bunch of people living up in Utah, or somewhere, who have lots of wives and do other crazy things. I'm telling you right now, I don't want to have anything to do with a bunch of wackos like that!"

I collapsed in a fit of coughing. Susan stared at me for a moment, and then without a word she got up.

"Joseph Altman," she said rigidly, "what on earth is the matter with you?"

I looked at her, scowling. "Nothing is the matter with me. I just don't want anything to do with a bunch of Mormons."

"You're wrong, Joseph," Susan whispered. "There *is* something the matter, and it doesn't have much to do with your terrible injury, either."

"So what is it?"

"The devil. Lucifer, Jesus called him. Nobody would ever talk like you just did, not unless the devil was right there working at him. If I were you, Joseph, I would think about what you just said, and how you said it. Then I would get rid of that evil creature!"

Then, with her head high, Susan turned and walked out.

# CHAPTER
# 18

After Susan had gone, I felt as miserable as a man can feel. I knew I had hurt her. Worse, I knew I had disappointed her deeply. Nor could I understand why I had reacted so strongly to her mention of the word *Mormon*. Back in high school I had known a couple of Mormons, and they had been all-right kids. So what on earth had gotten into me?

Perhaps Susan was right. Perhaps I did have a devil inside me. Or at least working at me. Maybe the only way I could work my way out of this was to pray. Only I had never felt so hesitant about prayer in my life. I felt totally unworthy, and I really struggled to do it.

"Dear God," I groaned as I stared at the ceiling, "if you're up there somewhere, why don't you just let me know? Things would be so much easier if I knew . . . "

Susan came back that night, and she and I had a long talk. I apologized to her, and after a tearful reunion of our hearts, she told me a little of what she had learned about what she was already considering as her new church. I was impressed, but I had several questions that she was unable to respond to. She had heard most of the answers but had simply forgotten them.

"Well," she said after we had visited for over an hour, "what do you think?"

That was a loaded question, for I truly didn't know. On the one hand, I was excited for what she was feeling. But on the other hand, I was unaccountably . . . well . . . *apprehensive* would be the best word. As I analyzed the situation, I feared that I didn't have the emotional energy to examine this new religion. Nor did I have the physical energy. What if the Latter-day Saint religion turned out to be like those evangelical radio ministries that Rence had talked about? Those folks had seemed to have all the answers. And they talked about Christ constantly. The trouble was, as Rence's mother had learned, most of them were more interested in building their own empires than in building the kingdom of God. Would it turn out that these Mormons were as hungry for power and money as those men were? I didn't know. Nor did I know how I would ever have the strength to decide. I was steadily growing weaker, and it was nerve-wracking to feel my life literally ebbing away.

"Joseph?"

I looked up. "Susan, I . . . I think what you have found is . . . wonderful. I want to learn about this church too, only I don't know how . . . I can."

Susan smiled. "Joseph, I asked the elders if they would come here tonight. They should be out in the hall by now. If you feel up to it . . . "

"Hey," I said, trying to grin, "that's great. I really would like to talk with them."

Susan squeezed my hand and hurried out of the ward to get her elders. And I wondered, as I watched her leave, if maybe I was crazy. I was so weak I could hardly move, and the pain was growing steadily worse. Yet amazingly, I *did* want to talk with those guys. If by chance they actually had the answers to the quest that I was on, then I could die in peace.

So I watched the door and waited, wondering with half my mind if I would be able to understand what these men would tell me, and wondering with the other half if I would be able to believe them.

A few moments later, when Susan introduced her Mormon elders, I almost laughed. And I would have, if I hadn't been so miserably ill. They seemed far too young to know about religion. And they *didn't* know everything, either. But they did understand quite a bit, and after I had asked them a few questions, I realized that I was becoming impressed.

Elder Stan Sharp was tall, dark, and already slightly balding, even though he couldn't have been more than twenty. Elder Ed Carlson was shorter and fair, and I guessed that he would go bald too, though it hadn't happened yet. Both men were from Utah, and they both had terrific timing with their humor. Elder Sharp's humor was crazily offbeat while Elder Carlson's was more serious, and I found myself almost enjoying our conversation. I couldn't enjoy it totally, however, for my dizziness was growing worse, and an unending feeling of nausea was coming at me like waves on the shore.

"Joe," Elder Carlson said easily, "Susan tells us that you and she are going to get married."

"Yes," I said, trying to clear my mind. "I guess she hooked me, all right."

"Man," Elder Sharp responded, holding his hand up like a claw, "sharp hooks here, if you know what I mean. But Susan's hooks look soft and painless."

"Well," I grinned weakly, "maybe they are and maybe they aren't. I've got enough pain elsewhere that I probably just can't feel them."

"Joseph," Susan asked quickly, "is it worse?"

"No," I hedged. "I don't think so. I'm fine, Susan."

"Are you sure? You seem terribly white to me. I don't—"

"Susan . . . I'm okay."

Elder Carlson then spoke. "Joe, if you'd like a blessing, we can give you one."

"*Blessing?*" I could remember Susan saying something about healing earlier that afternoon, but it wasn't clear. In fact, hardly anything was clear, except that I had a driving desire to question these men, to grill them until *I* knew whether or not they were Christ's messengers.

"Are you two faith healers, too?" I asked, doing my best to smile.

"Not exactly, though healing does come by faith. But we hold the priesthood of God and have the power to bless the sick, just like the ancient apostles and other saints."

More warning bells! But it wasn't the time for them, not now.

"No, thanks," I grunted. "I'm . . . fine. Susan says I can ask you some questions?"

"Anything you want. We'll try to answer them."

"Has she told you why I'm interested in talking to you?" I asked.

Elder Carlson nodded. "She told us about you, your two friends, and your list. She said you each agreed that you would search until you found the Savior's true religion."

"That's right, we did. But one of us is dead, and neither Jamie nor I have had much luck, at least as far as finding Christ's church is concerned."

"Maybe that luck is about to change. Do you still have your list?"

"I do," I responded, motioning toward my wallet, which was on the stand beside my bed. "There are seventeen evidences there, so you've got a real job ahead of you, responding to each of those."

The elders laughed easily, and then I continued.

"Susan, would you . . . mind getting the list out of my wallet?"

She smiled and complied, and then handed the dirty, creased yellow card to Elder Sharp.

"Good grief," he said softly, "this is a microscopic mess. I write small, but this is ridiculous. Are you sure this is English?"

"Actually," I smiled weakly, "it's hieroglyphics, a year and a half ancient. If you can't make sense of it, then maybe Susan can help you."

"No, we can figure it out, can't we, Elder?"

"You bet," Elder Carlson replied. "Just let me get out my urim and thummim."

"Your *what?*" Susan asked.

"Never mind," Elder Sharp replied. "You'll have to forgive my companion. It's a dumb joke he throws at me about once a day."

"Only when I try to read your minute scribbling," Elder Carlson countered.

"That's what I said. About once a day. You and Susan dug all these points of doctrine out of the Bible?"

"Well, not really *us*. The genius behind it, the man who really did the work, is my dearest friend. He spent about a year going through the Bible, and then we began to compile this list together. Before I met Susan, we had come up with fifteen points, and then she added another two almost immediately. Since then we have spent our spare time looking for a religion that has these doctrines in it. And there is an eighteenth point that isn't written down."

"Another one?" Susan exclaimed. "I haven't heard—"

"I forgot to tell you," I gulped. "I . . . found out this afternoon that Satan is just as real as the Holy Spirit is. I don't know any scriptures to support my point, but—"

"Actually, Joe," Elder Sharp said, "there are many scriptural references to Satan's reality. The Prophet Isaiah saw him cast out of heaven, and of course he appeared to the Savior during the forty-day fast preceding Christ's ministry and did his best to destroy the Lord. In reality, that's how Satan works. He attacks us at our weakest point. Your health is bad, Joe, so you can expect that he will use that weakness to try to get to you."

"Do I ever know that," I growled. "But I don't want to know about Satan, not now. I just wish that I understood more about God's methods of doing things."

"Joseph—"

"I know that Susan doesn't completely agree with my questioning, and I know that the Bible says that God is unchanging. But gentlemen, I've seen some pretty harsh things, pretty hopeless things, and I don't think I ever yet met anyone who really *knew* how to get through to God for help or comfort. I've met several folks who *claimed* they could, but when it came down to it, all they seemed to be doing was feathering their own nests, or wandering about in spiritual darkness with no idea that they were even lost. If God is there, then why doesn't he respond and show us his true way of worship—his true church?"

"That's a fair question. If you found a church that had each of these doctrinal points, would you be likely to accept their answer to it?"

"I . . . I don't know. Frankly, I'd probably doubt their veracity, their integrity. I'd guess they were making something up."

Elder Carlson laughed. "It *would* seem like it, wouldn't it."

"I don't think so," Susan declared quickly.

"But that's because you have a lot of faith and a certain naivete," I said. "You just haven't seen all that I have seen, Susan."

"I know, but—"

"Joe," Elder Sharp wisely interrupted, "what I believe you are saying is that you have three questions to which you have never found answers: Where did you come from before birth? Why are you in mortality? And, Where are you going after you die? Don't they summarize your questions?"

Well, if the warning bells had gone off before, now they were threatening to break out of my skull! Weisenburger and his friends *had* to have been Mormons! They'd asked exactly the same questions! And now that I thought of it, these elders had the same almost effortless feeling about life, as Weisenburger had had. In a way, they reminded me of my friend Will—possessors of a mighty secret that gave them an unbelievable advantage over the rest of the world.

"Would you like us to go down this list with you, Joe? We could do that, or we could tell you about how God has, at last, opened the heavens to a modern prophet named Joseph Smith and has brought about his 'restoration of all things' as prophesied anciently."

With an incredible sense of *déjà vu* I saw in my mind an elderly minister declaring to Rence Paxman and me not only that a restoration of all things had been prophesied, but that it was very near and indeed might already have taken place. I also heard us discussing the fact that we would surely recognize it if it had happened.

I thought of that and realized that I had been leaning on Jamie's list, feeling certain that *if* I ever found a church that taught such doctrines, those points would be my sign from God to believe. Now here it was, and already I was doubting.

How ridiculous! I almost laughed as I thought of what Satan was trying to do to me. To seek and seek until I had finally found, and then to immediately begin doubting. Talk about ludicrous!

"Elders," I said, though my waves of nausea were becoming higher, and I didn't know if I could ward them off much longer, "I would like you to go through my list. Would . . . would that be too much trouble?"

"Hardly any trouble at all," Elder Carlson said. "But Joe, do you feel well enough?"

"Whether I do or not, I've got to know! I've looked for so long, and I don't know how much longer I have."

"Joseph, don't talk like that."

"Susan, face it, will you? I'm in bad shape, and I've got to know if this church you have found is the one we've been looking for. I can't die until I know."

Susan, her face streaked with tears, squeezed my hand, and then without a word she arose and left the ward. That surprised me, but I put it aside and turned back to the elders.

"Before . . . you go down the list, I have two questions that I've thought about . . . for a long time. The first is simple. Does your church pass the plate? Or have the radio ministries that call for people to send in their money?"

"Absolutely no to the last question. And what do you mean by the first?"

"I mean that every time I visit a church, instead of building to a spiritual climax dealing with Christ's love, they end up talking about how much money I need to contribute to keep their ministry going. I just don't believe that Christ runs his church by using social pressure to get people to drop twenty-dollar bills into a silver plate."

"Neither do we," Elder Carlson responded. "And to answer your first question, we don't pass any plates. The

Lord has instructed us to pay a tithe, or ten percent of our income, to him. This is done with a sealed envelope in complete privacy, and it ends up being an issue of integrity between a man and his God.

"Oh, and one other thing. The money is used to build up the kingdom, by constructing temples and new chapels around the world, and by paying utilities and maintenance costs. None of it is ever used for salaries or personal profit."

"Thank you," I said while the bells rang again. "I'm glad to know that. Now for my next question. My friend Jamie Deltano told me that there would need to be another book of some sort in addition to the Bible. He said it would have to be scripture, but about a different people than the biblical population. Does . . . your church have such a book?"

"Yes, we do, Joe. It's called the Book of Mormon."

"And it is scripture?"

"Very much so. It is a history of sorts, and it deals with God and his relationship with the ancient inhabitants of America. It is sometimes referred to as the stick of Joseph."

"That's right! How did you know?"

"Joe, the prophecy is in Ezekiel chapter 37, verses 15 through 17. It is fulfilled by the Book of Mormon. That book is a record of the descendants of Joseph who was sold into Egypt. It is literally their 'stick', or scroll, or book."

"Amazing . . . Uh . . . I met a minister this past summer who said that point of ours about two books of scripture had to be wrong. He told me that the Bible says it can't be added to or taken away from."

"Actually, it says that twice," Elder Carlson stated, "once in the book of Revelation, and once in Deuteronomy."

"Well, if it says that—"

"Just a minute, Joe. You didn't hear me. It says it early

on in the Old Testament. If it had meant *not* to add any other scripture, we'd all have to throw away every verse of scripture from Joshua forward, including the entire New Testament."

"So . . . what do you think it means?" I asked, trying to concentrate.

"It means that we don't have the right to add to or take away from those particular books, which is exactly what the verses say."

"That's an interesting interpretation."

"Well, there are other things, too."

"Such as?" I asked.

"Such as the fact that there are seventeen books of scripture mentioned in the Bible that are not found in it."

"There are?"

"Yes. I don't know them all from memory, but there are some missing epistles in the New Testament. And in the Old Testament we know of the Book of the Wars of the Lord, the Book of Moses, the Book of Jasher, and so on. What if they were found? If you couldn't add to the Bible, what would we ever do with these books that the Lord's prophets considered important scripture?"

"All right, I give up. So *why* this Book of Mormon?"

"Joe," Elder Carlson asked, "are you sure you feel well enough for this?"

"I feel . . . fine, I tell you. Now, why the Book of Mormon?"

Elder Carlson sighed and looked at his companion.

"I saw that," I said, smiling weakly.

"We see you, too. Joe, you're sweating, and we mean rivers. Are you sure —"

"I want to *know!*"

"All right. The Bible is a sacred history of God's dealings with his children in Palestine. But he had other children —

other sheep, Jesus called them—who lived elsewhere."

Warning bells were sounding, and once again I was seeing Steve Weisenburger, listening to him grilling me about those other sheep that he claimed lived in America, and which I had had to admit, even then, looked like they had. I mean, *somebody* had lived on this continent back then, and they could have been Christ's other sheep as well as any other people.

"So, your Book of Mormon is the record of the . . . the Indians?"

"Well, they weren't called that back then. But yes, the book is their record."

"So . . . so how did Christ get here?"

"How do you know that he did?" Elder Carlson asked.

"A fellow I met once told me so," I replied. "Or I think he did . . . "

"He came after his resurrection," Elder Sharp said. "The account of that visit is in the Book of Mormon. Joe, we really need to let you rest. We have a copy of this ancient record that we would like to leave with you. Then, when you are feeling better, you can read it."

"And Joe," Elder Carlson added, "there is a promise in the very last chapter of the book. The Prophet Moroni, who wrote the last portion of the book, promises that if you will read and pray about it with real intent, God will tell you of its truthfulness. In fact, it says that through sincere prayer you can find out the truthfulness of *all* things."

"Sounds like a great promise. I know of at least one person who would surely like to know the truth of a few things."

Both elders smiled. "Shall we look at your list in order, Joe?"

I nodded, and so one after another the two Mormon missionaries went quickly through the list, citing facts, evidences, and scriptures. And I will say this — in spite of my growing physical distress, it was an impressive discourse. According to them, virtually every one of our points was contained within their religion. In other words, *everything* fit.

And that was where things stuck. To me, they all fit too nicely. It was inconceivable to me that a church organized exactly as Christ's had been and containing the same beliefs and practices could be so little known. I mentioned that, and Elder Carlson answered.

"Joe, do you remember how well Christ's church did when it was here upon the earth the first time?"

"Yeah, it grew pretty big."

"Yes it did, but only over many years. And how did the prevailing religions treat the Christians in the meantime?"

"Rough. Like I feel."

"Joe —"

"I'm . . . kidding, fellows. They were . . . persecuted. That's one of the items on our list."

"And that is exactly what has happened to the Mormons," Elder Sharp declared.

"You mean by not being accepted?"

"That and more. Joseph Smith, our first prophet, was murdered, along with his brother, and so were many of our members, then and in the years since. We were driven from town to town and from state to state until we finally came to rest in Utah, which was then a desert waste. And still today, despite our rapid growth, we are considered an anomaly by many other Christian denominations."

"Elders," I said, doing my best to grin, "I'll tell you this much — I think that Susan's a believer."

Elder Sharp smiled. "Yes, the Lord has given her a great understanding. He'll do the same for you, Joe. All you need to do is ask."

"He doesn't much talk to me," I said, laughing a little — because if I hadn't laughed I would have wept with pain and despair.

"If he doesn't talk to you," Elder Carlson responded gently, "it's because you haven't fully paid the price to know. Joe, there is actually a nineteenth point we need to add to your list, one that you and your friends somehow missed. In fact, I would say it is the most important evidence of all."

"What is . . . it?" I questioned, trying my best to focus on what he was saying.

"Just this, Joe. When you have had the fulness of the gospel of Jesus Christ presented to you, then the Holy Spirit is obligated, by the Savior's frequent promises, to bear witness to you that the gospel is *true*."

"In other words," Elder Sharp added, "you shouldn't take *our* word for this, or even Susan's. No man or woman can survive eternity on the witness of another. Your obligation and opportunity is to ask God if these things are true, for yourself. If you ask sincerely, exercising your faith, then he will respond to you personally. God *will* answer your prayers."

"Well," I groaned, "I certainly hope he does. I . . . I'm really losing steam, you guys. I . . . I don't know . . . "

"Joe, are you sure you don't want a blessing?"

I shook my head, careful not to shake it too fast. I didn't know what was happening, but it surely didn't feel as if it had very much to do with religion and my list. Deep inside me something was wrong, and I was awfully sick.

"I . . . I'm just tired," I mumbled. "Thanks, guys. I appreciate your time, and I think . . . I think it makes a lot of sense. What you say about your beliefs, I mean. Come see me again, will you?"

"We will, Joe. Let us know . . . "

I don't know what else he said, for I either went to sleep or passed out, I don't know which. All I know is that when I woke up, the elders were gone, I was on my stomach in some room other than the ward, and nurses were scurrying everywhere.

"What . . . what . . . "

"Don't talk, Lieutenant Altman. The doctor has been called, and he'll be here shortly."

"But . . . what is it? Why . . . "

"Shhh. Just relax. There's a little problem . . . "

Again all was darkness, and I spent a lot of time floating in it, happy to be free of my pain. Then the darkness was filled with the red of new agony, and I awakened, screaming.

"I'm sorry," a man's voice declared. "I know this hurts, but that's the last of it."

"Doctor," a woman's voice said then, "should we put him under?"

"No point in it. It's too advanced, and there's nothing more we can do."

I heard that, and I knew suddenly that I was dead. It had already happened, and I was beyond help. My next conscious thoughts, if indeed I would have any, would be in eternity.

In an anguish of desperation I tried to tell the doctor not to give up, but for some reason all I could do was mumble. I did, but no one paid any attention. They were too busy with my body.

I floated again, and somehow I was hearing the elders telling me that I had to pray. I tried, oh how I tried, but I couldn't concentrate.

"God," I cried desperately in my mind, "those missionaries said you would tell me . . . Please let me know . . . "

I floated again, and my mind seemed to be going to many other places. I was with Jamie and Will, watching the list being drawn up on the huge blackboard. I was kneeling beside the body of my friend Rence Paxman, wondering why he had to die. I was sitting on the airplane watching Steve Weisenburger smile back at me before he jumped. I was sitting beside Susan, thinking about the beauty of her spirit. I was relaxing on the lawn on the campus at Southern Cal, feeling foolish as Jamie chided me for my stubbornness.

"Joe," he was saying, "Joe . . . Joe . . . "

# CHAPTER 19

"Jamie," I mumbled, "leave me alone! I don't have to—"

"Joe, wake up!"

The voice, urgent, prodded at my consciousness, and I struggled to understand why Jamie would think I had gone to sleep. I hadn't! I had only—

"Joe, it's me . . . Jamie Deltano."

Pulling at my heavy eyelids, I finally worked them open. "Jamie?" I gasped. "Jamie, what . . . ?"

"Joseph?"

"Susan? I thought you had gone. I thought—"

"Joseph," Susan cried, "listen to me! I went to find the bishop, and Jamie was there with him. So I brought them both."

"Jamie? The bishop? You mean the *Mormon* bishop?"

"One and the same," Jamie declared, and I could see him smiling. "He and I gave you a blessing two days ago, Joe. Why do you think you're still here?"

"*You* gave *me* a blessing? But I don't—"

"Joe, the bishop is *my* bishop; the Mormon Church is

*my* church, and for the past two weeks I have held the holy priesthood of God. Now, just relax so we can give the Lord a chance to raise you up from this bed of affliction. In fact, now that you're awake to add your faith, I'd be happy to give you another blessing. What do you think?"

I nodded silently, and with tears of gratitude running freely, I lay with my hand in Susan's, while my dearest friend in all the world, Jamie Deltano, placed his hands upon my head and, in the name of Jesus Christ, and with Christ's authority, rebuked my illness and promised me a complete recovery.

# EPILOGUE

## The
## Present

# CHAPTER
## 20

"Y ou must have lived, Daddy," Marcie declared, teasing me a little.

"Quite well, too, in spite of the trials and tribulations you and the other children have inflicted upon me."

"Ohhh, poor Daddy."

"I wish your mother was still alive. She'd confirm it."

"So, Jamie had really joined your . . . the Mormon Church?" Arlene asked, obviously affected by my story.

"He certainly had. Almost three months before I returned to California, as a matter of fact. He had even written me about it. But with my illness and transfer, the mail had just never caught up with me."

"So, what was he doing with the bishop that night?"

"That was strictly coincidence, unless you believe in the same miracles I do. Jamie just happened to be with him when Susan arrived at the chapel. He had thought he had gone to the bishop's office for an interview. Personally, however, we all felt that the Lord had answered my weak prayers and had placed him there, just so he could help with that blessing."

"That's really neat," Arlene answered. "Doctor Altman, have you ever regretted it? Joining the Mormon Church, I mean?"

"What do you think, Marcie? Have we regretted it?"

"Oh, Daddy, of course not. Arlene, the Church has been the glue that has kept us together—especially while we were growing up without Mother."

Instantly, and without warning, I found my eyes brimming with tears, tears of loneliness for the companion of my dreams, and tears of joy with the anticipation of one day soon being with her again.

"And what about Mr. Deltano," Arlene quizzed. "Does your church still mean as much to him as it did when he converted?"

I thought of my friend, then, up in O.R., thought of his great successes and his terribly difficult trials, including his tragic divorce, and once more the tears welled up in my eyes.

"He loves the gospel of our Lord just as much as I do, Arlene, and I'm sure he has served it much better. And speaking of Jamie, if you girls will excuse me, I need to get upstairs to see how he's doing."

"Before you leave, Doctor Altman," Arlene said, "I want to thank you for taking time to share your experience with me. You see, I have been searching too. Ever since I can remember, I have been looking for the Lord. But I haven't ever found him . . . Uh . . . do you possibly have a copy of your list that I might borrow? I would be very interested in studying it over the holidays."

I grinned. "Sure do, Arlene. It's somewhat changed, though."

"What do you mean?"

"I mean, in the years after my wife and I joined the Church, we found several additional points, or evidences, that Jamie and the rest of us originally missed. In fact, the list now has forty-two points."

"You're kidding!"

"No, I'm not. But I want you to know, Arlene, that one of the original points is still the most important one for you to remember tonight."

"Which is?" Arlene asked.

"It is that you can know, through the power of the Holy Spirit, that The Church of Jesus Christ of Latter-day Saints is God's only true church on the earth today. I bear witness of that, and if you will approach the Lord in total sincerity, He will bear witness of the same truth to you.

"Now, if you'll both excuse me . . . "

Leaving Marcie and Arlene together, I took the elevator up to O.R. To my surprise, the room was empty. Stepping back into the hall, I was directed to a nearby recovery room.

Feeling guilty that so much time had elapsed since Jamie had gone into surgery, I stepped into the room, smiled at the nurse, and found Jamie already conscious.

"Hi, Joe . . . " he said weakly.

"Hello, Jamie," I replied, steeling my emotions against his obvious condition. "How . . . do you feel?"

"I . . . uh . . . weak, Joe. I can hardly even breathe. Other than that, I have no pain. I think that means I'm still . . . paralyzed."

"Well," I said with forced enthusiasm, "these things take time, Jamie. But I'll go in a minute and get a report, and then we'll know more. Doctor Thomas and I must have just missed each other when I came up."

"Joe, I . . . uh . . . "

"What's the matter?" I asked quickly.

Silently Jamie grimaced, his eyes closed, while beads of perspiration appeared on his forehead. Taking a deep breath, he opened his eyes and looked at me.

"I . . . I do have a little pain," he gasped. "And wouldn't you know it? It's in . . . my head. The . . . only place . . . where . . . "

At that point Jamie drifted off into the deep sleep that comes so easily following surgery. After waiting for a few moments to be certain that he would remain asleep, I left him in the hands of the nurse and sought out Dr. Thomas.

Briefly he gave me his analysis of the situation, and with heavy heart I made my way back to Jamie's recovery room. There was no hope at all, and it was only a matter of time, perhaps even minutes, until my friend's mortal life would come to an end.

For more than an hour I sat by his side, listening to the almost silent midnight sounds of a slumber-filled hospital. And as I sat, I found myself thinking once again of this great man who lay dying at my side. I thought too of Jamie's wonderful list, the list that had helped impel me into my marriage with Susan and into the only complete and true church of Jesus Christ.

Subconsciously, I reached into my back pocket and removed my wallet. From deep within one of the rarely used pockets I pulled a folded, yellow card. The creases were so permanent that as I unfolded them, portions of the card came apart. But it had done that before, in years past, and I had repaired it with tape. Now I would simply do it again.

Amazingly, the tiny writing was still legible. But even if it hadn't been, I would have been able to read it. For forty years I had had that list memorized, word for dynamic word, and I had never yet found a discrepancy in it.

"Evidences of a structured church," read the heading. And then beneath, under point one, was the doctrine of the Godhead, which consisted of the declaration that the three beings whom I worshipped were separate and distinct Gods.

I smiled, remembering Jamie's testimony to me; his emphatic statement that he was certain that what he had discovered, as evidenced by the baptism of Christ, was true. The three members of the Godhead were indeed that— three! God the Father, Jesus Christ his Son, and the Holy Ghost. It was almost as if—

"Do . . . you still have that . . . old card?"

Surprised, I looked to see Jamie awake and watching me, a ghost of a smile on his tired face.

"I'll have it until I die," I declared emphatically.

"I . . . still carry mine, too," my friend whispered. "As it . . . turns out, that is . . . the most important bit of . . . research I ever did. Daily I thank God that you and Will . . . and Susan . . . helped me to . . . find the Lord's church . . . I . . . Joe?"

"What is it, Jamie? I'm right here."

"Joe, look! She's coming . . . "

Quickly I looked around for the nurse, wondering why her appearance would make my friend so excited. But she had stepped out for a moment, and Jamie and I were alone in the room.

"Jamie, the nurse is gone, but she'll be right back, I'm sure."

But Jamie was ignoring me, his attention and his eyes focused on a point somewhere beyond my left shoulder.

"Susan," he whispered while I stared at him. "I didn't expect to see you . . . Oh, already? But I haven't finished . . . Oh, I see. Yes, I know. Look at him. He even has my old card. Now that is dedication . . . "

"Jamie," I said as I reached out and took his nerveless hand. "Jamie, do you see Susan? My Susan?"

Jamie's eyes flashed as he looked at me. "Of course I see her," he responded instantly. "She's standing right here. You can see her too, Joe. All you need to do, is . . . Oh, we need to go? But . . . Susan, who is that beside you? I can't . . . "

And then I watched as Jamie's questioning look was replaced by one of the happiest, most sublime expressions I have ever seen on the face of another human being.

"Will?" he beamed. "Will Huckstedder, you old atheist! Oh, you're not? Well, that's fantastic! Then are you with Susan? . . . "

Now I stared behind and about me, while the old bells tingled and my body quivered with the certain knowledge that my limited mortal vision was preventing me from seeing things as they really were in that hospital recovery room.

"Jamie," I said as tears coursed down my cheeks, "tell Susan that I love her and . . . miss her! And tell Will how proud I am that he had the courage to keep searching until he too found the Lord . . . "

But Jamie couldn't tell them, at least not from beside me. When I looked back at him, I saw that his eyes were fixed, that his spirit had already gone. My eternal companion and my two dearest friends were no doubt rejoicing together in that eternal kingdom of the Lord Jesus Christ, which is open to all who will repent and be baptized by proper authority, just as the Holy Spirit had witnessed to me so many years before.

# Forty-two Evidences of the True Church of Jesus Christ

Henry L. Whiffen, a dear friend, has independently developed a separate work identifying thirty-two points or evidences of the true church, with extensive references. Twenty-three of his points overlapped our research, which added nine additional evidences or points to our list. In his work, he has written the following: "If you were to look at a set of blueprints for a building, it would identify all the details of one specific structure that would generally not be exactly identical to any other building anywhere. There may be others that are very similar, but because of the individual detail required for a particular location, a specific set of plans will fit only one building.

"The God of this earth has performed a phenomenal feat through His creation of all the necessary elements of our existence — the galaxy in which our earth revolves; the sun, moon, and stars, which give us light, heat, control and season, and even monitor the tides of the ocean; and the existence of all plants, animals, minerals, and elements, without which we could not live. And, of course, the creation of our magnificent bodies themselves is a marvel beyond our comprehension.

"All of this has been done by careful plan and design for God's purpose, which is to clothe our spirit with a body that will enable our spirit to grow, gain additional experience in mortality that could not be obtained without bodies, learn to overcome the weaknesses of the flesh, and progress to the point where we can live once again with God.

"God's plans are very specific, just as an architect's plans for a building are specific. In order for God to help us understand how to live (so we can return successfully to Him afterwards), He has taught the prophets down through the ages and commanded them to teach all the people of the earth. These teachings, the doctrine or gospel of salvation and eternal life, have always been consistent because God's plans are still exactly the same. In order to keep this consistency or uniformity of God's true gospel, His true church has been established and maintained among faithful people throughout the ages.

"Down through the ages, Christ's words have been interpreted many different ways by many different people. As a result, hundreds of churches have been started, to teach the different interpretations of Christ's gospel, and there is even much disagreement *within* churches as to interpretation. Since the teachings are often very different and directly contradict one another, they cannot all be right—which means there is much being taught by many churches that is incorrect.

"With so many churches not having the completely correct gospel of Jesus Christ, how could an individual find the true church? Fortunately, the Bible can help answer this question. Just as an architect's plans for a building are specific, and are exactly right for only one structure, so also are God's plans for His true church. He has said, 'Strait is the gate, and narrow is the way, which leadeth unto [eternal] life, and few there be that find it.' (Matthew 7:14.) However, a careful reading of the Bible will clearly identify specific characteristics of Christ's true church."

We agree with Mister Whiffen, and so present the following. The evidences or points are not arranged in any particular order, and the scriptures listed are, in most cases, only a sampling of what may be found within the holy writ.

## The Evidences or Points

1. The Godhead consists of three separate and distinct beings — God the Father, his Son Jesus Christ, and the Holy Ghost.

> Genesis 1:26-27; 3:22
> Matthew 3:17; 28:19
> Luke 3:22
> Acts 7:55
> 1 John 5:7

2. God the Father, as well as his Son Jesus Christ, who is a resurrected personage, both have bodies of flesh and bone and spirit.

> Genesis 32:30
> Exodus 33:23
> Luke 24:39, 41-43
> John 20:17; 21:13-14
> Acts 7:55-56
> 1 John 3:2

3. Jesus is the Christ, the literal Son of God, the Messiah, and the only perfect person upon the earth — and not simply a great teacher.

> Luke 9:35
> John 17:4-5

Hebrews 1:6-7

4. Jesus Christ, as revealed in the New Testament, is Jehovah, God of the Old Testament.

Exodus 3:14
John 8:58
Isaiah 43:11
Hosea 13:4

5. The Holy Ghost is a distinct personage of spirit and is the third member of the Godhead.

Matthew 3:15-18
John 14:26; 16:13-14; 20:21-22
Ephesians 1:17

6. The Holy Bible is the word of the Lord insofar as it is translated correctly. It is the record of the Jews and will be joined with another record in the last days to relate God's word to his people. This second record will come from a descendant of Joseph.

Ezekiel 37:15-17
Isaiah 29:18
Revelation 20:12-14

7. Jesus Christ is recognized as the head of his Church, with other officers named, beginning with a foundation of apostles and prophets, and including teachers, saints, elders, evangelists, bishops, deacons, priests, and high priests.

John 15:16
Mark 3:14-15
Ephesians 2:19-20; 4:11-14

8. Officers in Christ's church will be "called of God." They will receive their authority through "the laying on of hands." One cannot call himself to the ministry.
   a. College degree or license insufficient
   b. Royal priesthood will be known as such

   c. Bishops and leaders are to marry and to have children

      Acts 19:25
      Hebrews 5:4, 10
      Timothy 3:2; 4:2-3
      1 Peter 2:9

9. Members of Christ's church will be "workers," and will be called "saints." In addition, women will be included in activities and leadership.

      Proverbs 12:4
      Romans 1:7
      Ephesians 4:12
      1 Corinthians 11:7
      2 Thessalonians 1:7-10

10. There will exist within the church separate entities for each of the groups of members. Adult and youth organizations will exist. This point stands to reason, if Christ is concerned with helping each individual from that person's own level of understanding.

      Ephesians 4:11-14

11. Christ's church will believe in the "virgin birth" of Jesus Christ but will not believe in the "immaculate conception" of Mary.

      Isaiah 7:14
      Matthew 1:19-20, 23
      Luke 1:26-31, 42

12. Christ's church will believe in immortality or eternal life, and in a heaven and a hell. After the resurrection, we will be assigned to different places according to the judgment. The first resurrection will be for the righteous and will commence 1,000 years before the second resurrection.

      John 3:16-17; 5:28-29; 14:2
      1 Corinthians 15:20-22, 40-42

1 Thessalonians 4:16-18

13. The Savior's church will honor Sunday as the Sabbath, with the understanding that the resurrection transpired Sunday morning, the first day of the week — and thus replaced Saturday as the Sabbath.

Hosea 2:11
Matthew 28:1
John 5:18
Acts 20:7
1 Corinthians 16:2

14. Officers as well as members of Christ's church will receive continuous revelation from God.

Amos 3:7
Matthew 16:13, 16-19
Ephesians 1:17

15. Members of the Lord's church will be payers of tithes and offerings.

Malachi 3:8, 11
Luke 11:42
Hebrews 7:4-5

16. Members of the church will regularly partake of the Lord's supper. This sacrament represents the flesh and blood of Christ and is partaken of in remembrance of him.

Matthew 26:26-28
Acts 20:7
1 Corinthians 16:1-2

17. Members of the Lord's church will experience miracles, such as visions, tongues, and prophecies. In addition, the church will practice divine healing. When members of the church are sick, elders of the church will anoint them with oil and heal them.

Matthew 9:18

Mark 6:5; 16:17-18
Acts 5:12, 16
James 5:14-15

18. Church leaders will teach that the resurrected Jesus Christ will come again to the earth in the last days. This "second coming" will be greatly anticipated.

Job 19:25-26
Matthew 24:30
Acts 1:11; 3:19-21

19. Members of the Lord's church will be persecuted for their beliefs.

Matthew 5:10-12; 24:9
Luke 6:22-23
Acts 8:1-3; 28:22
Hebrews 11:36-38

20. The church as a whole, as well as its members, will be recognized for their "fruits"—as will the prophets who lead them. The church will esteem honesty, virtue, and wholesome activity.

Proverbs 15:4
Luke 6:43-44
2 Corinthians 9:10
Philippians 4:17
Hebrews 13:18

21. The church must provide salvation for *all* of God's children, not just those who receive the gospel while living on the earth. It will practice baptism for the dead.

Mark 16:16
John 3:1-8
1 Corinthians 15:29

22. The church will build temples similar to the one Solomon built, which was destroyed and built again at the

time of Christ. These temples will have unique purposes, including baptism and other ordinances. Temples will also be holy places, contain the Holy of Holies, and be used by members as places of worship.

> Isaiah 2:3
> Malachi 3:1; 3:7

23. Christ's original church was organized by him and named after him, and his church today will also be named after him.

> Acts 4:10-12
> Ephesians 1:22; 4:11-14; 5:23-24

24. Specific authority to function in the administration of the church is called "priesthood." It is obtained through ordination by one having the power to so ordain.

> 1 Samuel 13:9-14
> Mark 6:7
> John 7:16; 20:21
> Acts 19:2-5
> Hebrews 5:4-6, 8-10

25. A higher priesthood authority is required to bestow the Holy Ghost than to baptize.

> Matthew 16:19
> Mark 1:7-8
> Acts 8:15-18; 19:2-6

26. The church that Christ originally organized did not baptize infants since the prerequisite for baptism was (1) a capacity for repentance of past personal sins, and (2) a personal belief in the divinity and teachings of Christ.

> Mark 10:14-15; 16:16
> Acts 2:38; 8:12

27. The church is to send out missionaries (in twos), to preach the gospel of Jesus Christ.

Mark 6:7
Luke 10:1

28. The church will have a welfare system to provide for the poor and the needy within the church. Members are to provide for themselves and their families first, and then receive help from the church.

Deuteronomy 15:11
Psalm 9:18
Isaiah 14:30
Mark 10:21
Luke 18:22
Romans 15:26

29. The church will have a law of health. Alcoholic beverages will not be used by members of the church.

Ephesians 5:18
1 Corinthians 5:11; 6:9-10

30. The church will be one that is restored to the earth. Christ's original church experienced a great apostasy or falling way, but his church will be returned or restored again in the last days.

Jeremiah 31:31-34
Acts 3:19-21
2 Thessalonians 2:1-13
Revelation 14:6-7

31. Christ's church will believe in being saved by the grace of Christ through exercising faith in him. In other words, it will teach that when we repent of our sins and forsake them, the atonement of Christ will cleanse us of our sins.

Matthew 7:21-29
Mark 16:15-16
Luke 6:46-49
1 Timothy 4:10

James 1:22-25; 2:14-26

32. The church will preach only the true gospel of Christ, with no variations. It will neither add to the meaning of Christ's teachings nor take away from them — even though current revelation will provide insight into them.

> Matthew 5:19
> Galatians 1:6-9
> Ephesians 4:5
> Hebrews 13:8-9

33. Christ's church will espouse a pre-earth life, or a pre-existence, such as that taught by the Orothodox Jews. Included in this teaching will be the doctrine of foreordination and not predestination. God the Father will be recognized as having created the individual spirits of all people.

> Genesis 1:26-31
> Job 38:4-7
> Ecclesiastes 12:7
> John 17:5
> Ephesians 1:4-5
> Hebrews 12:9

34. The church will believe in the "original sin" of Adam. Nevertheless, it will teach that Christ atoned for Adam's sin, and that we will be punished for our own sins, as Adam's sin has already been atoned for.

> John 1:29
> Acts 24:14-15
> Romans 5:6-19
> 1 Corinthians 15:21-23

35. Christ's church will teach that the gathering of Israel, in the last days, will be literal.

> Isaiah 5:26-30; 11:12-13; 35
> Jeremiah 3:14-18; 31:10

36. Members of the true church will respect the beliefs of others and will allow all people to worship as they choose.

> Galatians 5:22-26; 6:1-2
> 2 Thessalonians 1:7-10

37. The church will be subject to the laws of the land, regardless of the type of government in power in that land—thus rendering to Caeser that which is his, and to God that which is his.

> Matthew 22:21
> Mark 12:17
> Luke 20:25

38. It should be recognized that, while perfection is to be sought by each member of Christ's church, the members will have human failings and will make mistakes, and they will thus need to grow and learn—line upon line, precept upon precept.

> Isaiah 28:10
> Ephesians 4:11-14, 28, 32

39. After repentance, baptism by immersion is essential, as is receiving the gift of the Holy Ghost. A person performing these ordinances of baptism and the laying on of hands for the gift of the Holy Ghost must be duly authorized to perform such ordinances.

> Matthew 3:13-15
> John 3:5
> Acts 2:38, 41; 22:16
> Romans 6:5-6

40. The Savior's church will have an unpaid ministry. This lay ministry will be called "by revelation," even as the apostles called new members to their quorum following the resurrection of Christ.

Amos 3:7
Micah 3:11
John 10:13
Acts 1:22-26
1 Corinthians 9:18
1 Peter 5:2

41. Satan is a real spirit being and not a figment of people's imagination.

Job 1:6
Matthew 4:10
Mark 1:13; 8:33
Luke 13:16; 22:3, 31
John 13:27
Acts 26:18

42. The Holy Ghost will bear witness of the truthfulness of the Savior's plan, when it is presented. This is the one sure way of knowing which, if any, of the churches belongs to the Savior.

John 16:13-14
1 Corinthians 12:4-12
Galatians 5:22-26
Ephesians 1:17